IRISH COUNTRY PEOPLE

Irish country people

KEVIN DANAHER

THE MERCIER PRESS
4 BRIDGE STREET, CORK

© Kevin Danaher, 1966
First published 1966
Reprinted 1969
Reprinted 1976

ISBN 0 85342 057 2

Reprinted Photo-Litho in the Republic of Ireland

Contents

Note: The series of articles brought together in this book first appeared in *Biatas*, published by Comhlucht Siúicre Éireann Teoranta; they are republished here with the approval of the editors of *Biatas*.

By the same author:

In Ireland Long Ago
Gentle Places and Simple Things
Folktales of the Irish Countryside

Country Childhood

The day was never long enough for all the things we wanted to do. Half a mile above the house the heather grew on the hill, half a mile below was the river, and between the two and on them and in them was our ranging ground. Too small and too unskilled to handle a *sleán* or a turf-pike we were mere brief onlookers at the turf-cutting on the hill bogs, soon wandering away to explore the mountain, to hunt for elusive lizards or to raise a grouse or a woodcock and tell each other what we could do if only we had a shotgun, and wandering back again to share the workmen's tea and bread and cold bacon. In the early summer, when the turf was being saved, even unpractised hands were useful at stooking, and we often joined in the work, usually making a game of it, seeing who could build a stook fastest or produce the most elaborate or fantastic effect, only to tire of it in half an hour or so and wander off in search of something more adventurous, or be chased away by some expert to whom our artistic efforts did not appeal. Then there were all the fields between the edge of the bog and the river, and we were free to roam them, for we knew the respect due to hedges, gates, gaps and growing crops. Often we dammed a small stream and teemed the water out of the holes lower down to see if we could catch a trout; this was a race against the water rising above our weir of sods and stones, for, as often as not, our frantic effort to empty the pool was defeated by a gush of muddy water. Sometimes we fished the river pools with proper fishing rods, but generally found this too contemplative a recreation and laid the rods aside to sail *feileastrom* boats, paddle in the shallows, swim in the deeper pools or explore the river banks. Eel hunting with its rushing and shouting was more to our taste than fly fishing. Equipped each with a table fork 'borrowed' for the occasion we turned up the stones in the shallow water and stabbed any unfortunate eel thus disclosed. There was an old-fashioned type of table fork with three prongs, made of hard steel with a bone handle; the prongs of this, unlike the nickel-plated variety, could be rubbed needle sharp on a smooth stone, and then heaven help the eel that came the way of the lucky wielder of one of these weapons. When we could lay hands on a couple of planks to make a raft or when we succeeded in smuggling a wooden tub away from the house, we boldly set sail on the river, and if we were fortunate enough to have two vessels afloat at the same time we fought spirited naval actions which usually ended in the complete submergence of one or both crews. Fortunately no one was ever drowned.

There was hardly a tree, a bush or a plant which did not provide us with some amusement. A stalk of green corn could be made to produce a most fascinating noise; cut off short above a joint and with a slit about an inch long cut downward below the joint it could be put into the mouth and blown like a reed. These we called *deocháns*, and to hear five or six of them with different and discordant notes all being blown together would break the heart of any musician and delight that of any small boy. An old workman showed us how to make sycamore whistles; with a good deal of careful cutting and tapping the bark could be slid off a short length of sycamore twig and then replaced when the twig had been cut to the proper shape, to produce a piercing whistle, very useful for signalling to each other or calling up help in wild games of cops and robbers. A length of elder branch, laboriously cleared of its pith, made a most useful tube. It could be turned into a flute or a popgun or a water squirt, as could the more fragile but more easily cut stems of angelica and similar plants. We were expert at plaiting rushes. The long ones which grew on wet ground made most useful whips, and a couple of dozen pieces about a foot long could be bound around with longer rushes to make a baton, which we knew by its old Norman-French name of *bastún*, and used freely in mimic fights, knowing that its contact with the head of a contemporary gave a most satisfying sound without causing any great damage.

We knew the whereabouts of every wild fruit over two or three square miles of countryside: crab-apples, sloes, damsons and *fraocháns*. There were three or four cherry trees near the ruin of an old farmhouse, and these we looked upon as our private preserve. We knew where the best ash plants and blackthorn sticks could be found, and frequently made ourselves new walking-sticks and lost them just as frequently. One of us read somewhere that acorns could be roasted and eaten, and we were lucky not to have poisoned ourselves in experiments with these and other growths which we thought might be good to taste. We knew where the biggest horse chestnuts for conkers could be gathered. And of course the trees themselves gave endless scope for climbing and acrobatics, for building huts in and for swings; our favourite swing had only one rope, with a short strong stick tied at the lower end, for this not only swung back and forth but also could be made to twirl round most excitingly.

Like all boys we loved to throw things. A pile of stones with an old tin can on top made a fine cockshot, and we spent happy hours 'croosting' one of these from a set distance, letting the smaller boys stand nearer to give them fair play in throwing. Another game was to designate a stone as a mark, or 'jack' as we called it, and pitch other stones towards it to see who could come nearest without actually hitting it. Then there was 'skinning the cat', that is skimming flat stones on the surface of a river pool. The bow and arrow was, as far as I know, never a traditional plaything in our district, but we learned how to make and use them in archery contests and Red Indian games. We tried hunting with them, with arrows carefully feathered and tipped with a sharpened nail. We even made a crossbow, a very deadly weapon with a spring steel bow which shot darts made of short lengths of umbrella rib, but when our parents discovered that this engine could drive one of the darts through a sheet of corrugated iron, it was impounded and an edict issued for its abolition before anyone was killed. And one bright boy, who had dipped into an illustrated Roman history book, designed a slinging engine of the ballista type which could throw a sod of turf a full hundred yards. I can still remember every detail of its making, but, in the interest of disarmament, refrain from divulging them. Catapults had come into use in the district fairly recently, and the earliest ones which I remember had the rubber tubing used for babies' bottles as springs. Later the favourite material was strips cut from a motor tube. Some of us were really expert with the catapult. One of my cousins could cut the head off a thistle ten times out of ten at a range of twenty yards; he had devised his own particular form of ammunition, small metal discs made by breaking the stems off boot studs. Formerly the casting weapon of the district was the sling, which was made from a small piece of soft leather – the tongue of an old boot made a very good one – to which were fastened two lengths of cord about thirty inches long. A small stone was laid on the leather and the user, holding both strings by the end in his hand, whirled the sling round his head and slung the stone by letting go one string at the right moment. We tried this, but never became good shots. But some of the older boys, when I was very small, were remarkably expert. I saw one boy loading his sling with a piece of slate and hitting a bird in flight so hard that it was cut in two. The force of the slung stone was frightful, and I can well believe the tradition held in the locality that slings were used as weapons in battle in former times.

In these days of teeming motor transport the crossing of any road, even in the remoter corners of the countryside, needs caution, but in the middle of the nineteen-twenties cars were few and far between and the road was as much our playground as were the fields. Tar macadam and concrete were only beginning to appear on the more important main roads; the other roads were repaired by filling the holes with broken stone which was gradually ground into dust by the iron tyres of the carts so that there was dust in summer and mud when it rained. When the mud got too deep it was brushed and shovelled into the broad margins at the sides of the road, and the margins, made fertile by the horse droppings cleaned from the road, usually had good grass and luxuriant wild flowers. Because of the grass it was customary in many parts of Ireland, and in our district among them, that a cottier who had no land could keep a cow by allowing it to graze on the roadside. While near the cottier's house an occasional eye to the cow was enough, but when farther away she was usually in charge of a child. These herding children were our friends and we spent happy hours helping to 'mind the cow'. One of our favourite games on the road was skittles, which was played with six short lengths cut from a tree branch two or three inches in diameter. They were sawn cleanly across so that they could be stood on end. A square of about two feet was marked on the road, and five of the pieces were stood upright on it, one at each corner and one in the middle, while the sixth was the missile to be thrown at them. You got one point for knocking down one of the corner skittles and three for the middle one. Marbles was another game which needed a hard surface, and when we played marbles, which was seldom, we played on the road. When we could lay hands on a barrel hoop or the rim of an old bicycle wheel we played 'bowleys', trundling the wheel along with a short stick. The lid of a tin can, nailed through the middle to a stick about a yard long could be trundled along too, and a superior version of this was made from an old bicycle wheel; this wheel on a stick was known by the peculiar name of 'joodelum', and with them, as well as with the 'bowleys' we ran stirring races along half a mile or so of road that sloped gently down hill. We cut pieces of cardboard into propellor shapes, tacked one of these on a stick and ran along with it so that it spun around in a most fascinating way; one handy boy used to carve propellors from wood, and these were much better than the fragile cardboard spinners. A boy from the far end of the parish showed us how to make stilts by cutting a pair of stout saplings each with a short projecting stump at a suitable height, and these went much better on the road than on the soft and uneven surface of a field. As to races on foot and on bicycles, the road was best for these. Of course running on a road was not without its minor risks; we were allowed to go barefoot in the summer, and the contact of a bare toe with a loose stone might leave the owner of the toe limping for a couple of days. Bandaged toes were no unusual sight.

When we could round up half a dozen donkeys we ran donkey races, or played hurling on donkey-back which took no little skill without saddle or bridle. And no knight of old ever went into the lists with greater zest than we; armed with sweeping brushes couched like lances, we tried to unseat each other from the donkeys who often added to the fun by lying down and refusing to take further part in the melée. All this had to be done without striking the donkey, which was considered very bad form.

The day was never long enough for all the things we wanted to do, especially when broken by school, homework and other such annoying interludes. We were never bored; anywhere and anytime we could find some pleasant occupation or other. Toys and books and comics were all very well for the winter evenings, but our chosen playground was outdoors and our playthings the things we found there. Looking back I find myself being sorry for the city children of today who are so much cut off from that world of adventure. Recently I heard a story: the uncle said to the small boy 'when I was your age I sailed down the river on a home-made raft' and got the answer 'If we had a river and if Daddy bought me a home-made raft, I'd go sailing too.'

The Widow's Curse

In many parts of Ireland the tale of the widow's curse is told. Usually it is a sad story, a story of greed and cruelty, of tragedy and retribution. A poor travelling woman, a young widow with a little sick child is pitied by the kindly neighbours and they build her a little cabin and bring her food and milk. Then the landlord, a hard-hearted man, hears of it, and orders his henchmen to throw the widow out and burn her little house. And so it is done in harsh winter weather. The child dies of the hardship and the distracted mother lays a solemn curse upon the landlord and his house – for seven generations not one of his male heirs will die in his bed, and seven widows will be left with young children. And so it comes to pass – we hear of deaths by suicide and on the hunting field, in battle and on the sea, until the seven generations have passed.

Down on the fertile plain of County Limerick there is a certain castle, a tower house of the late fifteenth century, standing grim and gaunt over rich pasture land. About two hundred years ago a substantial farmhouse was built beside the castle, and in this house there lived about 1790 an elderly widow and her only son. She was a bossy old person who tried to run her son's life as well as her own, and when he fell in love with a neighbour's daughter and married her against his mother's wish the old dame feared to cross him openly, but being skilled in the laying of *piseóga* she took secret measures against the young pair, speaking a dreadful curse upon them. Never, she said, for a hundred and fifty years, would a child be born in the house upon which the shadow of the castle fell. By an unfortunate chance there were two other farmhouses on which the baneful shadow fell, and they, too, came under the malediction. The young couple grew old and died childless, and the farm passed to others, and so it went on, year after year in all three farms; never once was the cry of an infant or the laughter of a child heard in them. Until at last the years were fulfilled and a child was born in one of the houses – the house of the old hag – in the nineteen-forties. And when the old people of the place learned that the attendant doctor was the grand-nephew of a couple who had lived childless on the same farm they felt that the tradition had been perfectly rounded off and all the harmonies of folk belief preserved. In another way, too, the proper sequence of events was, according to the old people, fully maintained. For, they said, an evil curse did no good to the one who laid it. Only the curse of the innocent and the afflicted brought no evil upon those who uttered it. 'Wait till you see, now. Curses come home to roost. *Fillean an feall ar an bhfeallaire!*' And they told, in hushed voices, how the old woman of the castle farm never had a day's peace in her life again and, in the end, died a gibbering lunatic.

Once I came upon a man who was solemnly cursing

those whom he regarded as his enemies. He had a grudge against the world and spent much of his time and all of his money in drinking his grievances into a coma. Returning home one evening he was assailed with a shower of clods by some corner-boys, and in his rage he cursed them. First he strewed some small stones on the road. Then he drew up the legs of his trousers and knelt bare-kneed on the stones and began to pour out a long litany of curses.

– 'That ye may never have a day's luck! That all belonging to ye may die with the hunger!! That yeer eyes may fall out of yeer head!!! That yeer guts may tie in a knot!!!!....' and so on and so on. But the unseen marksmen were not unduly worried by his maledictions; they kept up a shower of missiles which grew heavier as time went on until at last he had to retreat defeated. Such outbursts lay as lightly on the cursed as did that of the wandering gentleman whose 'Dublin watch and chain and seal were stole away in Doneraile' and who reviled the robbers in verse, or the effusion of Mistress Nell Flaherty of Coothill on hearing of the loss of her pet: –

'May his pig never grunt! May his cat never hunt!
May a ghost ever haunt him at dead of the night!
May his hen never lay! May his ass never bray!
May his goat fly away like an old paper kite!
May he swell with the gout! May his teeth all fall out!
May he roar, yell and shout with the painful toothache!
May his temples wear horns and his toes many corns,
The monster that murdered Nell Flaherty's drake!'

It is true, indeed, that Irish poets were seldom behind-hand in mockery of their enemies. The satire, the poem of mockery, was a powerful weapon in ancient times, and many a rich man was moved to reward a poet not so much from appreciation of his art as from the fear of hearing abusive songs about him sung by the whole countryside. And it was only a short step from verbal abuse to curses, thus the poet's curse was well known and often feared. People have had the feeling that there was something magical about poetry, that the poem itself as well as the poet had some occult power for good or for evil. The poets were not slow, in ancient times, to take advantage of this, until their exactions from rich and poor alike became unbearable. One early tale tells us of a large group of poets and their hangers-on coming to the palace of a king, demanding all comforts. Among other things each was to have a bed to himself, with another bed beside it at a slightly lower level, so that if he happened to fall out of bed during the night, he fell into the lower bed! No wonder that the poets were sentenced to banishment from Ireland, and that only the pleading of the great Saint Colmcille saved them. As long as rural poets wrote in Irish the poet's curse kept its strength. Some years ago the last Irish speaker in the Galtee mountains repeated for me with great vigour the lines in which a poet had called down wrath on the corpse of a local tyrant two hundred years before: –

'Thaiscídh, a chlocha, fé choigilt i gcimeád criaidh...'
'Press down, ye stones, tightly in binding clay,
That treacherous, blood-stained boor, Dawson the grey...'
which ends –

'That ravening greedy worms his corpse may rend,
That his soul may roast in the pit for years without end!'
and even yet one can find verses of this kind made and sung.

If we are to believe the old tales, the saints themselves were moved on occasion to vent their displeasure in curses, and, we are told, the curse may still operate. Saint Patrick cursed the wretch who stole his goat to make a drum of the skin – and the distant throbbing of that ghostly *bodhrán* is still to be heard along the Boyne on a still night. Saint Ita spoke against the idlers who tormented the little donkey that carried her milk churns – That their boorish conduct might never be forgotten! – and there is a village near the borders of County Kerry where still the taunt is heard: 'Who threw the stones at Saint Ita's ass?' Sometimes a holy man, in awful anger, uttered a dreadful malediction and then repented his haste, but the curse had gone forth and could not be unsaid, so the saint took to his prayers and diverted the harm elsewhere. Saint Mo Lua was enraged by the conduct of the people of Ardagh, and declared that never a Sunday would pass without one of them being stretched dead outside the church, but when the people begged forgiveness and promised to mend their ways the good saint transferred the curse to the birds of the air – and ever since that day a dead bird is found near the church in Ardagh every Sunday of the year. Likewise with the inhabitants of a certain part of Donegal when Saint Colmcille despaired of ever leading them to virtue and cursed them root and branch. One of his followers begged him to moderate his anger and in the end succeeded in having the curse changed to the rushes that grow in the fields, as a proof of which you have only to examine any clump of rushes and you will see that the tops are always withered by the curse.

The blacksmith had strange powers, among them the power of cursing evil-doers. In laying the curse the smith would solemnly lift his anvil and turn it around. Clergymen, too, of all denominations had the power of reading from the 'book' and calling down misfortune upon incorrigible sinners; they could, for instance, cause the miscreant's feet to adhere to the ground so that he could not move. There is the story of the Parish Priest and the rude little boy. 'Come here, sonny, please, and hold my horse a minute for me' 'Faith an' I won't not hould your oul' horse!' 'You rude boy. Don't you know that I could stick you to the ground?' 'And if you're so smart, why don't you shtick the oul' horse to the ground?'

In many parts of the country there is a tradition that curses were laid at blessed wells. Ordinarily a person making the 'rounds' walked around the circuit of the well clockwise, 'with the sun' as the old people said. But in calling heaven's retribution on those who had wronged the innocent, the rounds were made lefthandwise, 'against the sun', and instead of blessings all sorts of calamities were prayed upon the head of the enemy. This was not to be undertaken frivolously, for the old rule held – the curse had to fall somewhere, and it could recoil on him who spoke it if his own conscience was not clear, or if he was not certain that the one he cursed had done him grievous wrong and was unmoved by any decent feeling. In ancient times there was a good reason for cursing the oppressor. The law often operated in a way which seems unjust to us, for although a man might have gone to a learned brehon and had his rights made clear to him, there often was no machinery for the enforcement of the law and the vindication of his rights. If he had powerful friends, well and good, but if he was poor and weak he might go whistle for justice although clearly in the right. In such a case a solemn, public curse might move the wrongdoer to repentance and restitution. But, said tradition, the plaintiff must clearly show his own probity and innocence; thus it was held that he who laid the curse must be quite sure of the justice of his cause and must, when actually pronouncing the curse, be in the state of grace and fasting since the midnight before. Then his prayers for justice and vengeance would be heard.

In several localities in the north and west of Ireland there were special places where curses could be laid. One such place was Kilmoon, not far from Lisdoonvarna, where certain stones near the ruins of the old church had the power to cause the mouth of the one cursed to turn crooked. These stones lay on top of a wall under an old tree beside the blessed well of Kilmoon, and the curse was laid by going fasting to the well, saying certain prayers and then turning the stones while naming the one to be cursed. Even fifty or sixty years ago people had a horror of such a curse, and it is recorded that a certain farmer of North Clare, when brought to court for striking a beggar-woman, pleaded that it was in self defence as she had threatened to turn the stones against him, and the magistrate accepted his plea and took a lenient view of the case. At Kilcummin in County Mayo an ancient gravestone caused those cursed upon it to become mad, and, we are told, a local man at the beginning of the last century derived a small income from laying curses there for a fee. The cursing stones of Ballysumaghan in County Sligo brought tragedy to a local family. The man of the house missed a firkin of butter from his dairy, and accused a neighbour of stealing it. The neighbour loudly proclaimed his innocence, but the angry owner rushed away to the stones and prayed that the thief might be struck dead. Returning home he found his wife and his son afflicted by some strange ailment which carried them off in a couple of days, and he learned that his wife had been in debt unknown to him and had, with the help of the boy, abstracted the butter and sold it at the market. The famous stone on Tory Island could bring down a storm on those cursed and was, we are assured, a defence and protection to the Islanders in the old days, for if danger approached they could call up a tempest to drive the ships of the invaders away.

During the nineteenth century the notion of the solemn curse on one's enemy gradually died out. The clergy spoke out strongly against it and several cursing stones and similar objects were destroyed by the local priest or minister. And the coming of justice in the place of oppressive law has removed the ancient need for solemn malediction of evildoers. Our ancestors were mightily afraid of curses, but we can afford to regard them as no more than a piece of bad manners.

The Tailor

In the old days in the Irish countryside, and, indeed, up to quite recently, men's clothing was made to measure by the tailor. Readymade suits were not normally for sale in the shops; a certain amount of second-hand clothing might be bought from travelling stall-holders at fairs and markets, and a certain amount of readymade new clothes was available in seaport towns for the fitting out of sailors just landed from long voyages, but the ordinary man or boy had his measure taken and his cloth made up by tailors who always were themselves men. Women's clothes, on the other hand, were often made by the housewives themselves, while the finer items, costumes, gowns and cloaks were made by the country dressmakers or 'manty-makers' who were, of course, women. When this custom of men tailoring only for men and women for women came into the Irish countryside, we do not know. It appears from what little evidence we have that in ancient times all clothing was made by women, and that many of these were very expert in the decoration and embroidery of garments as well as in the fashioning of them. It seems probable that tailorings as a man's craft began in the medieval towns and spread from them into the countryside; the Irish form of the word, *táilliúir*, which comes from Norman French, appears to confirm this. In any event the traditional tailor of the countryside is a man who makes clothes to measure for men.

In the towns and the larger villages you had resident tailors with regular workshops, often master tailors with a number of assistants and apprentices. Out in the country the tailors were most often journeymen or travelling craftsmen who put up at one farmhouse after another, staying in each until all the necessary clothes were made and then going on to the next house. Because of the sedentary nature of the work, the tailor was often a small, pale, sallow complexioned man, contrasting unfavourably in physique with the outdoor workers and the burly artisans such as the wheelwright, the sawyer or the blacksmith. Often, too, a youth with weak or injured legs or similar disability found this no disadvantage in learning the trade, and this, too, helped the notion of the tailor as a small, weak man. And his craft, which appeared rather womanish to more robust workers – many of whom might be jealous of his fine skill, his ready earning capacity and his position in the rural community – helped to set him apart from other workers. Many of the tailors developed a bossy attitude, insisting that everything should be just as they wanted it, not only in the matter of the cloth and thread provided by the household, in which any sign of poor quality led to a series of disparaging comments by the indignant craftsman, but also as regards the food and accommodation provided for him. His taking of the measure was ceremonious, and the man of the house had to turn this way and that and hold up or extend his arms endlessly until the finicky expert was satisfied. Usually too, he ingratiated himself with the women of the household, sitting all day on the kitchen table busy with needle and scissors, retailing all the news and gossip of the countryside and keeping up a stream of light and pleasing conversation. He was a travelled man. He had served his time in a town and had much to tell the country cousins about town ways. Often he was an expert storyteller or ballad singer, and you might be sure that the neighbours gathered in the evening in the house where he was working to be entertained by him with news, song and story. No wonder, then, that he cut quite a figure and that he became the centre of much tradition.

We often heard the story of the journeyman tailor who was awakened early on a May morning by sounds from the kitchen. It was in the loft over the lower room that he had been given his bed, and he was surprised at the bustle in the kitchen because the day had scarcely dawned. He peeped out and saw the woman of the house drawing water in a wooden can and filling a big tub. Next she threw in what appeared to be herbs and followed this with a coal of fire. Then she undressed, jumped into the tub and changed in the twinkling of an eye into a hare, and away out the door with her. Half an hour later back came the hare and was changed again into a woman by the magic tub. The tailor, drawn between fear and curiosity, gave no sign of what he had seen but worked away cutting and sewing all day. Next morning the ceremony was repeated, but no sooner had the hare-woman rushed from the door than the brave tailor had his nightshirt plucked off and had plunged into the tub, and away with him in pursuit of the other hare. Soon he arrived at the top of a little hill where many hares were gathered and waiting. Then came an ancient, venerable hare to preside over the unholy meeting, but the old hare came forward and announced in a human voice: 'Home with you all! There is a stranger among us!' The hares scattered in all directions but the tailor had kept his eye on the woman of the house and followed her closely. Two yards in front of him she was in the door of the house, and the moment she stepped out of the tub she overset it, spilling the water, and it was only with a frantic dive that he plunged into the saving brew. Needless to say, he made no delay in dressing and gathering his things and leaving the house and the parish as fast as his legs could take him. He arrived at a house where he had promised to work, and although he was not expected on that day he was made welcome. He breakfasted and set to work on their new clothes, but out in the day, when the children came back from school, one inquisitive lad asked him what was that funny thing on his neck, and to his horror he found a small patch of hare's fur growing on the back of his neck – in the one place where the spilling water had not touched – a patch which remained there for the rest of his life. We can be sure that he kept to his bed until called from that day onwards, especially in the month of May.

Then there was the story of the little lame tailor, busy at his work, when the young mother asked him to have an eye to the infant sleeping in the cradle until she went for a sitting of eggs to a neighbour's house. He kept very quiet, in dread he might wake the child, but before long the month-old baby sat up and took out a little fiddle from under the cot-clothes and struck up a lively tune and the poor tailor found himself dancing a hornpipe, lame leg and all. The sound of the mother lifting the gate latch put an end to the music, and all was quiet when she came in to the kitchen. After a while the tailor drew her aside and questioned her about the infant, did she notice anything strange about him? Yes, she said, it was very queer, but for the first three weeks he was the lovely quiet child, always happy and satisfied, but for the last week she could get no good of him, always whining and getting weak and sickly so that you'd think it was a different child entirely. 'Come in with me now, ma'am' says he, 'I won't hurt nor harm him, but you'll see what you'll see.' In he went, and got the tongs and put it into the fire until it was red hot. Then he stood in front of the cradle, in sight of the child. 'Do you know what, ma'am' says he, 'but the best way to cure a puny sickly child like that is to catch the bad in him with a red hot tongs and pull it out of him. And that is what I am going to do now.' And with that he waved the hot tongs over the cradle. Up with the thing out of the cradle and away with him running out the door like a hare, and the tailor hobbling after him waving the tongs, and the poor mother with every 'Dia lem' anam!' out of her. 'And now listen, ma'am, to know would you hear a child crying' says the tailor. It wasn't long until they heard the fine healthy cry of a small child out in the haggard. Out with them, and there was the lovely infant lying on a *beart* of hay, her own fine child that the good people had taken away. And the thing in the cradle was an *iarlais*, and only for the tailor it would have pined away and pretended to die and be buried, so that the fairies could keep the real child for themselves.

It was said that a good tailor would finish a suit of clothes in two days, but most people found that it took a little longer than that, about three days. One old workman told us that he took a piece of cloth to a tailor in the morning when he was going to work, and his new trousers was ready for him in the evening when he was coming home. The tailor provided the thread, buttons and pocket linings, and gave him back twopence change out of two shillings. An older man, one of the ancients of the parish capped this by telling us of the suit made for him as a young man. In this case the tailor provided all the materials and making, and our friend bought a new shirt from the change and still had one and ninepence to spend out of a pound which his father had given him to fit himself out for a journey. This brings up the tale of the miser. He was not prepared to pay the tailor what he owed him for making a suit of clothes without haggling and bargaining and loud complaints. In the end the tailor said 'I'll tell you what, sir; if you let me see all your wealth I will be satisfied with that and you need pay me nothing.' Well and good, the miser agreed to the bargain, and took the tailor into a strong room and opened a big chest that was closed with many locks and chains. And there was a great heap of gold. The tailor looked at the gold and then laughed long and heartily. 'What do you find to laugh at in my great wealth?' says the miser. 'My friend' says the tailor 'you have been gathering that gold for more than fifty years, pinching and scraping, working hard day and night, and starving yourself and your family to get it. And now I have seen it, and I have had just as much value from it as you have, because you never do anything except look at it.' And the miser understood what was meant, and he paid the tailor fair and honestly, and was a generous man from that day forth.

Tailors were talkative men, and the strange pair who worked once upon a time in our village were long remembered. Not one word would they speak to each other from end to end of the day, and to others they spoke only when it was absolutely necessary. One evening the two of them, master and journeyman, were seated on their bench, sewing away. It was the custom of many tailors to work in their stockings, and to have their shoes beside the table, ready to put on. On this evening, when several men were in the shop, the journeyman arose without a word, put on his shoes and walked out. Nothing was seen of him for nearly half a year, and then one evening he walked in again without a word, laid his shoes beside the bench and sat up and crossed his legs. The master tailor said nothing, merely handed him an unfinished waistcoat, which he took and began to sew. Nobody ever heard where or why he went, but all agreed that this was a most untailorlike silence.

Is minic says the proverb *do gheall táilliúir agus nár tháinig*, it is often a tailor promised and did not come. The tailor, said the people, would promise everybody that their new suits would be ready by a certain day, and often the day came and no suit was ready. But it was the tailor's pride that if an important occasion such as a wedding, or, more particularly, a funeral was to hand, the promised suit would be ready even if he and his workers had to stay up all night working on it. In some parts of Ireland it was customary that a dead man's best suit was worn three times to church on three consecutive Sundays and then given to the poor. In a few districts of the south-west an entirely new suit had to be made by the tailor, who had a record of the dead man's measurements, and worn on the three Sundays. In this event the tailor was most particular to have the suit made in time and exactly to measure, even though the ceremonial wearer might be of an entirely different stature and build to his dead kinsman.

It was said of many tailors that they were too ready to keep any bits of cloth left over from making a suit. Indeed it was said that many a tailor had enough material over, after a visit to a farmhouse, to make a complete suit for himself. 'It is often you'd know your own piece of material on him' said the sceptics. And we heard of the jolly parish priest who heard these tales and who said that no tailor would steal cloth from him. In due course the tailor came to the presbytery, and his reverence had a fine bolt of black cloth ready for him. The tailor took the measure and laid out the cloth and snipped away, and the priest looked on at the whole operation and took away every scrap that was left over. In due course the priest's suit was all sewn and ready. Now the priest and the tailor were of similar build, and imagine his reverence's astonishment the next Sunday when he sallied forth in his fine new clothes to encounter the tailor also taking the air in an equally handsome suit of black broadcloth. 'I give you best, I admit defeat' said he, 'But you must tell me how you got away with it under my very eyes.' 'That was simple enough, Father. All I did was to double the cloth, and for every bit that I cut for you there was a bit underneath cutting for me.'

The tailor's symbol was the needle. Before the coming of modern techniques of manufacture the making of a fine needle was a difficult work of art, and even a coarse needle was beyond the skill of the ordinary blacksmith. Thus needles were valuable; we are told in a passage of the Brehon Laws that the compensation to be paid for the loss of a needle was a heifer, and that for a fine embroidery needle an ounce of silver. By the time of the travelling tailors the value had fallen considerably, but they were careful of their needles, carrying them stuck in a row in a strip of cloth, which was usually kept safely in a little wooden case. The needle itself was not without power; if you pointed a needle nine times at a wart the wart was cured, but if you pointed the eye of a needle towards somebody you could wish him ill-luck. If somebody stuck a needle in a card-player's coat unknown to the player, his luck at cards would be good, and a needle in the dress of an unbaptised infant protected it from abduction by the fairies. When a man was setting out for the fair, his wife would put a needle in his greatcoat to bring him luck in buying and selling.

When travelling from place to place many tailors walked, but others, especially those who were 'weak in the legs', had a donkey and cart to carry equipment and personal belongings. While most of the tailor's gear, needles and thread, tape and scissors, were light, there was one heavy item, the 'goose' or large flat iron used in pressing the garments. Some tailors did not use this, but these were only rough workers, and any tailor with pride in his craft brought his 'goose' even if he had to walk from house to house. Some demanded that the farmer should send a cart for him and his gear, but usually they were content to be welcomed at the house door and made free of the kitchen until the work was done. Some of them followed a regular circuit, and the time of their arrival could be foreseen fairly closely. Others rambled at will, looking for casual work and sometimes quarrelling with the man on whose beat they were trespassing.

The travelling tailors no longer go their rounds, and even the town and village tailors have less to do than formerly, since so many men and boys now use all sorts of readymade garments, some of which, in style and colour, would astonish and dismay the craftsmen who served our grandparents so well.

The Feet - Water

In every farmhouse and *bothán* in the Irish countryside, the people, in the old days, washed their feet before going to bed. There were no high rubber boots then, and the 'low shoes' which were the ordinary footwear gave only limited protection against muddy roads, while for work in bog and tillage and farmyard, any shoes strong enough to protect the feet of a hardworking man were good enough; they were often worn without stockings, and a bit of muck on the feet did not matter. Besides, many people, especially children and younger people, went barefoot much of the time. Hence the necessity of washing the feet at night, a duty performed by all except the depraved or the eccentric recluse. Many houses had a special small wooden tub for feet-washing, others used the ordinary clothes-washing tub, and, in the poorest houses, failing other utensils, the three-legged pot was pressed into this service too.

Feet-washing over, the vessel of dirty water must be taken outside and emptied with care into the channel, for it was unlucky either to keep it inside overnight or to fling it through the door regardless of the possibility of drenching someone, human or otherwise, approaching the door. We all have heard tales of how the good people of the hills have power over the feet-water, and how it gives them entry to any house where it is kept in at night; we all have heard the story of the fairy women of Sliabh na mBan and how they were banished from the house by the clever girl who cried out that their mountain was on fire. This belief and its associated tales probably had its origin in nothing more mysterious than the simple rule of hygiene which demands that dirty water be thrown away. Old Irish custom demanded that fresh warm water for washing and for bathing the feet or the whole body should be ready without delay for a visitor; this was an essential element of hospitality, and failing to provide it was a serious breach of good manners. The guest who found a vessel of dirty water left over from the former user was grossly insulted; the ancient tale of the wandering scholar,

Mac Con Glinne, enumerates the deficiencies of the monastery guesthouse of Cork, unaired and verminous bedclothes, dirty water in the bathtub and nobody to wash his feet, no food and drink ready, all these equally slovenly and reprehensible.

There is a story about a man who was going the lower road west from the village one night, when he saw the figure of a woman standing by the side of the road and recognised her as one who had been dead these ten years. But, although the hair was standing on his head, he summoned up enough courage to ask her what she wanted. 'Look at me' said she, 'all soaked and scalded with hot water and dirty water and the dregs of the teapot. When I was alive I had the wicked tongue, and many is the time I said the bad word about the woman in that house there. And my purgatory is to stand outside her door from nightfall to dawn every night. And she is always flinging out water without a word of a warning. And, for the love of God, will you tell her to say something before she flings it out, and give me time to shove to one side or the other and not be soaked and scalded every second turn by the cold slops and the hot water!' The man took the message, and ever afterwards the housewife made sure to call out 'seachain!' or 'chughaibh an t-uisce!' when throwing out water or slops. And there was another story of the headstrong girl who would not be said or led and who 'didn't give in to them ould piseógs' and refused to call out the warning when she was throwing out the water. Until one night when she threw out a big keelerfull and was slapped across the face by a hand which was invisible, although the print of the five fingers on her cheek was visible for days. Some people held that, as an additional precaution, a small hot coal from the fire should be dropped into the vessel after use; the fire banished any evil influence. This must be done in the case where, owing to shortage of hot water, two people had to wash their hands or feet in the same water; the first user dropped in a little glowing coal, and the water was thus cleaned for the second. Some people held that it was sufficient if the second user spat in the water before using it. And let us not affect disgust at this use of spittle. In many parts of the world it is considered a good and lucky thing to spit on an object or even a person to bring good fortune or ward off evil; spittle was used in cures, too – did not Our Lord Himself cure the blind man with spittle?

Before the days of the modern bath, and of its predecessor the movable metal bath-pan, washing and bathing vessels were of wood, nearly always cooper-made hooped tubs of different sizes. In fine weather adults bathed in the stream or river, rubbing themselves over with soap before splashing around in the water. In winter time the adult's bathtub was a barrel, economic of hot water, and it is more than likely that the bathing vessels mentioned in such ancient documents as the Brehon Laws were barrel rather than trough shaped. Children were bathed in a smaller wooden tub before the kitchen fire. It was said that Mary bathed the infant Jesus in such a tub, and there is a story about that, too. During the flight of the Holy Family towards Egypt, and with Herod's murderers on their track, they asked for shelter one night at a lonely cave out in the desert, where there was a woman with a small child of her own. She gave them food and drink, and a party of rough-looking men, who arrived soon and ate supper in the cave, paid no heed to the fugitives. Mary and Joseph knew that they were desert robbers, but that poor people like themselves had nothing to fear from them. Soon the woman of the cave heated some water to bath her baby, but seeing that Mary's Infant was dusty from the journey, she offered the tub of hot water, saying that her own child was afflicted with leprosy and the healthy baby should be washed first. But when she put her child into the water that had washed the Holy Child, the leprosy vanished and her little son was cured. And that child, grown to manhood and a robber like his father, was the Penitent Thief of Calvary.

Nothing was more refreshing, said the old people, than to wash the hands and face in running water, but, of course, to wash the face, or the whole body, in dew, particularly the dew of May Morning, was the surest method by which a young girl could get a beautiful complexion. Stubborn dirt or grease could best be washed off the hands in the hot water strained off from boiled potatoes, and for hands dirtied by work in the bog or in boggy soil, bog water was much better than fresh water. The hair was washed frequently, especially by the women, who wore their hair long; the poets sing in praise of long hair, raven-black or red, gold or amber, in plaits or tresses reaching to their ladies' waists or knees or ankles. The men's hair style, on the other hand, varied; sometimes it was worn shoulder length and sometimes closely cropped. There were times when male hair fashions came under the scrutiny of the law; in the Middle Ages the Anglo-Irish parliament passed laws against anybody in the territories of the Pale following the Irish fashion of a fringe of hair on the brow or a flowing moustache. It is not recorded that the shorthaired men called the longhaired ones 'sissies', but we do know that Cromwell's followers in England were nicknamed 'Roundheads' and the Irish of 1798 called 'croppies' because of short hair styles. Baldness was a blemish; in the old Fianna tales Conan the Bald is a figure of fun, and Cuchulainn, when his hair was shorn off by his enemy Curoi Mac Daire, remained in hiding from his friends until it grew again. Both men and women carried combs to dress their hair; we read of the ladies, in ancient times, equipped with little ornamental bags which held their combs and cosmetics, these latter including eyebrow dye made from blackberry juice and rouge coloured with the sap of elderberries. Barbers and hairdressers are mentioned in the ancient literature, and it seems that some of them were experts of repute and position.

Beards, which had been out of fashion for some two hundred years, regained popularity about a century ago – our mental picture of a Fenian of 1867 includes a manly beard. The change of fashion was in some degree due to the Crimean War, but more to the American Civil War; the men on active service had little time for shaving and let their beards grow, and the beard became the mark of the fighting hero. A glance at a picture of the local football or tug-of-war team of sixty years ago will show that the beard had gone out of fashion again, but that the neat waxed moustache was the mark of the sportsman. Shaving and haircutting also had their share of curious belief. Men did not care to shave on Sunday, and did it on Saturday night. A vow never to shave on Friday, in honour of the Crucifixion, ensured good health, and there must be no haircutting or shaving on Good Friday. Some of the old people believed that they must have all their hair on the Day of Judgement, and when they had a hair-cut they gathered up the hair and hid it away safely, and similarly with clippings from fingernails.

Soap was made at home. Ferns and some thistles were cut and saved like hay, and then burned to ashes. The ashes were mixed with water and animal fat; goose grease was, they said, best of all for this purpose. Chemical change in the mixture produced soap which was put in small moulds to solidify, and we are told that it was very good soap. Fern ash, by itself, was also used for washing both the person and the household laundry. Starch was made at home by a process as simple as that used for soap. Potatoes were grated and stirred up in water and left to settle; the waste came to the top and the starch was deposited on the bottom, and when this had been again stirred up and left to settle in clean water it produced a very strong starch, as many an elderly man wrestling with a knife-sharp stiff collar on a Sunday morning would testify with emphatic verbal ornamentation.

The laundering of clothes was a vigorous business, and few of our vaunted modern fabrics would stand up to the boiling, scrubbing and beating to which the homespun woollens and linens were subjected, or to the long bleaching spread on lines or bushes. Clean clothes for young and old was the rule on Sunday morning, and the housewife took pride on how handsomely the menfolk and the children were turned out. The men's collars and shirtfronts must be as white as snow and as rigid as a board, and woe betide the little boy who dirtied his Sunday clothes, at least until he got home from Mass. Last week's dirty laundry was the main task of the housewife's

Monday, and the men might have to be content with a scratch dinner if the big pot was busily boiling the wash, and what with steam and flying soap suds and hot smoothing irons, it was much better to stay out of the house entirely. The larger items, sheets and blankets and so on, were dumped in a suitable river pool, well soaped and then walloped most vigorously with a *slis* or bittle, on a suitable flat stone. Many villages and towns had special places on the river bank where the women congregated to do their washing and where cheerful gossip and laughter mingled with the smack of the bittles. Thus the modern 'laundrette' of the towns, where for a small fee a woman may have the use of a washing machine, and a chat with the neighbours while waiting, is – apart from the modern appliances – nothing new. Use of the river, in the old days, was, however, free.

The Mason

Nobody is quite sure as to when the mason's craft was brought into Ireland. There are pieces of dry-stone walling to be seen in ancient tombs which may be three thousand years or more old, and some of the great stone forts, such as Dun Aengus or Staigue are generally held to have been built about two thousand years ago, but these have no mortar, and the art of the mason, as we understand it, is the erection of buildings of mortared stone. It appears that most of the houses of ancient Ireland were made of timber. Saint Bede the Venerable, writing about the year 730 A.D., describes a church at Lindisfarne built by Irish missionaries about a hundred years before his time, as 'of hewn oak, in the Irish manner', and an early life of Saint Patrick tells of how he came to a place in the present County Mayo and built a church with walls of earth because there was no wood near at hand. The earliest known Irish buildings of stone and mortar are small churches of some twelve hundred years ago, so we must conclude that the knowledge of mortar came to be known in Ireland about that time, probably brought in from

Continental Europe under the influence of progressive churchmen. These earliest churches are very simple structures, little more than four walls, but their still standing ruins show how good was the masonry and how skilled were the workmen. The larger churches of slightly later date show a further development of skill, both in the laying of mortared stone and the carving of fine ornament, with arches, lintels and stone roofs all eloquent of the masons' art. Finest of all of our early stone buildings are the round towers, and the men who built them must have been as well versed in the principles of architecture as in the laying of stone upon stone. Perfectly proportioned, soaring a hundred feet or more into the air, every stone carefully selected and shaped and set in place – these are buildings of which any country might be proud.

With such fine early work before our eyes we need not wonder at the proliferation of fine stone building in medieval Ireland, at the wealth of churches, castles and abbeys whose walls still stand in spite of storm and lightning, fire and gunpowder. We can only regret the fact that we know so little of the men who built them. We read that such a church was built by this bishop and such a castle put up by that great nobleman, but we can be sure that neither his lordship the prelate nor his lordship the earl laid hand to a shovel or a hod or a trowel during the building, and we may guess that their advice and comments to the craftsmen were more hinderance than help. But of the master masons and their workers we know next to nothing. An occasional name or record of payment in an old book, no more than these and of these hardly any – that is all. There are, of course, legends, some of them as tall as the round towers themselves. How this church tower could not be completed because an evil hag caused each day's work to be cast down during the night until the prayers of a saint prevailed against her. How dozens of bullocks were slain so that their blood might give strength to the mortar of this castle – and here we may hope that prime beefsteaks gave strength to the toiling masons. How the poet Cearbhaill

Ó Dálaigh, who had been nourished in infancy on the milk of a magic cow and thus had gained all skill and knowledge, confounded the masons who mocked him by carving a cat with two tails on the cornerstone of the building on which they were engaged. And, of course, of the prince of all masons, the Gobán Saor who invented mortar, who first showed how to 'break a joint' and to span a wide gap with interlocked timbers, and who, on a hint from his clever daughter-in-law, produced the mason's plumb and line.

That same Gobán was not very happy about his only son and heir. A strong, cheerful and willing lad by all accounts, but not among the intellectual giants of the period. Not exactly bright, if the whole truth be told. The only thing for you, my lad, said the old man to himself, is a clever girl for a wife. He had his eye on a neighbour's daughter who seemed to be clever as well as comely, and as luck would have it the young hopeful was not averse to the company of a pretty lass. 'Here is a sheepskin for you' said he to his son 'which you must take to the market, and you must bring back the skin and the money too', knowing well that the girl would be at the market and that his son would look for her sympathy, and hoping that she would rise to the occasion. Sure enough, evening brought the boy home with a smile as broad as a well laid doorstep, the rolled-up skin under his arm and the money jingling in his pouch, for the clever girl had made short work of shearing the skin and selling the wool for him. And so they were married, and that was the lucky day for Gobán senior as well as for Gobán junior.

It was not long after this when word came to the Gobán that the King of England wanted the finest castle in the world built for him, and who could build the like but the Gobán himself? Off he went with his son, walking before them with their tools on their backs. 'Tis a long road we have before us, son, and you must shorten it for us' quoth he. 'In the name of Heaven, how could I do that?' says the son. 'If that is the way with you, we might as well be turning home' says the Gobán. The puzzled youth did not fail to consult his wife, and as usual she set him right, for the next morning they set out again and this time when the old man told him to shorten the road he struck up a cheerful marching song, and so after many days they arrived in London town to find everything ready for them, heaps of the finest stones, loads of good lime and sand and dozens of workmen all eager to help the great master. For a year and a day the work went forward until at last the Gobán set the last pinnacle on the highest battlement, but as he stepped back to admire his work the king's butler, a friendly man with whom he had cracked many a joke and many a bottle of the king's canary wine, put the whisper in his ear. Treachery was afoot; the king was afraid that some other king might get the Gobán to build even a finer castle, and was planning to kill both him and his son that very night. In with the Gobán to where the king was sitting on his throne, planning further villainy. 'This for a story' said he 'We're nearly finished, but for one tool I must have, and by your leave I'll go back home with my son to get it. It will take the two of us to bring it, it is so precious and so important.' 'I'll send over for it and you can be putting a fine touch here and there to the castle while you are waiting.' 'But you'll have to send the best of men for it. Send your own son and I'll be satisfied that it is in good hands,' said the Gobán. And so the prince set out and a soldier along with him – he wasn't sorry to get away from the old devil of a king for a while. And the Gobán gave him directions, where to go and what to ask for. This tool had a very queer name – 'Twist for turn and turn for twist' – but the young wife got the message. 'Below in the cellar it is' says she 'and you must go down and get it yourself'. Down he went, and with that she banged the trapdoor on him. 'And now, my man' says she to the soldier 'back with you to the king as fast as your legs will carry you, and tell him that unless my men are back to me by the first boat, it is how he'll have his son's head for an ornament for the top of his new castle!' And I tell you that it wasn't long until the father and the son were home again.

In most parts of rural Ireland the mason's craft was hereditary and father was followed by son in the trade. Many of the masons were jealous of their knowledge and would allow nobody except another mason or an apprentice to see the finer work such as building an arch or 'drawing in' a chimney, so as to preserve the secrets of the art. All the materials for the building had to be provided by the owner, and the craftsmen were very particular about their quality and very critical of any shortcoming. I knew one old mason who drove to his work in an ass-cart, and whenever he saw a suitable building stone on the roadside or in the field he acquired it without delay; this was his craftsman's prerogative and nobody dared to object even when the stone was pulled out of a fence. Nice even stones easily dressed with the hammer is what he wanted, and they should be about six inches thick for good work. Corner stones and through stones, and stones for lintels, thresholds and water-tables were selected with care, and woe betide the man who had ordered the building unless these were forthcoming. Lime and sand for the mortar had to be of the best; even the water used to mix the mortar must be just right – if there was only bog-water in the place the owner must provide a cart and barrels to bring good water from the source indicated by the finicky craftsman. The country mason was his own architect, at least as far as concerned the building of the ordinary farmhouses; there were consultations with the owner on the matter of size and cost, and then the mason laid out the foundations and went ahead with the building. His tools were the age-old trowel, hawk and mortar-board, line, square and plumb-rule, mason's hammer and mixing shovel, and the real genius of his art lay in the mastery of his hands over simple materials and implements. Each morning he began by setting the corner stones; each evening it was his pride to finish off a complete course of masonry. No skimping for him, no botched, hurried work, no downing of tools at a set time, but always the patient, unhurried skill of the old-time craftsman.

The rural mason was a house-carpenter, too, doing all

the structural timber work of the building, and laying the slates if the farmer's purse and pretensions ran to a slate roof. He laid the flagged floors of the kitchens and the cobbles of the hearth and the drip channel around the outside of the house. He set the doorsteps, floored the byres with cobbles and built the farmyard walls. The building of gateposts and the precise hanging of gates was his special pride; the gateposts were of mortared stone and the gate was wrought by his brother craftsman, the local smith. If the farmer wanted a gate which swung closed when released, he made it so; if it should remain open he tilted it to the exact angle required. Few features of the Irish countryside show such nicety of combined craftsmanship as the old farm gates, and we cannot but regret that so many of them must be removed because of the increasing size of modern farm machinery.

If lime was scarce or difficult to get, an old-time mason was quite ready to build with clay-mortar, and although this did not bind the stones as securely as lime-mortar it was not a bad substitute. Not too many years ago, I saw a two-storied farmhouse being built with stone and clay-mortar, and more than one church has been so built. Failing all kinds of mortar, the mason was capable of very good dry-stone work, and with good stone this could be quite sound and durable. But all of these were held to be much inferior to the stone and mortar which were the mason's chosen material, and were used only in default of the better. The mason could handle the finest of materials as well as the worst, and where the owner could afford it he did fine plaster and brickwork. Many masons were also competent stonecutters, and made handsome fireplaces, window and door surrounds, cornices and ornaments, and where he was himself not an expert the mason always knew where a stonecutter could be found. When a bigger job, such as a bridge, a church or a large mansion, was planned, masons assembled to do the work. Like most tradesmen they were divided into classes according to their skill and experience. The master-masons were resident in the various areas and the apprentices lived and worked with them, but the professional masons who had not yet attained to the master's rank, the journeymen, were, perhaps, the most numerous, and wherever a big job was on hands the journeymen came from far and near, to work there for a longer or shorter time and then to pass on to some other job. Many of these wandering masons never reached the master's grade and never settled down. I knew one of these, although he was more a stonecutter than a mason; I remember him as a little, bent old man with a wisp of beard, getting weak and feeble but still with skill in his hands. He had a little cart like a perambulator in which he pushed his kit of tools before him along many a mile of the roads of Munster, and although he died in the county home when I was a small boy, his work is still pointed out and he is named as the man who carved it. The masons at work on a big building always made room for one of these travelling craftsmen, and if he showed skill he was sure of employment on the job.

The masons, like the exponents of most crafts, were very much a brotherhood. They were not as firmly organised as the trade guilds of the middle ages, but they had the bond of shared skilled and secrets. This is shown most clearly by the fact that they had a secret language of their own. The general form and grammatical structure of this was that of Irish Gaelic in most parts of Ireland, but some of the masons from English speaking parts used an English framework. But the vocabulary was the same in both cases, and a mason who knew no Irish could talk to one who knew no English in *bearlagar na saor*. Some of the words were Irish words said backwards; the word for small was *geab* (Irish *beag*), that for a horse *lapac*, and these gave *geablapac*, a pony (i.e. *capall beag*). But most of the words seem to bear no resemblance to those of either English or Irish, *Éis* = *man; bua* = *woman; airig* = *mason; airig fliúc* = *carpenter. Biniú the buá dacín for tís a caidhne, for carna* = ask the landlady for something to eat, for meat. *Coistriú go dtí cín a díogla* = come on to the public-house; here *cín* = house and *díogla* = drink. One mason told how, one evening in their lodgings, two journeymen were short of the price of a drink and one said to the other, in the presence of the unsuspecting woman of the house, 'Coistriúmíd to the cín an iarr with the lócan longshuain of the buadacín', which meant 'Let us go to the pawnshop with the landlady's bedclothes'. In the old masons' proverb 'Caid ar chaid, caid idir dá chaid, agus caid os cionn dá chaid' the only secret word is *caid*, a stone, and its meaning might be easily guessed by the unitiated, but a phrase like 'geab do luadar' dropped casually by a mason identified him to a brother mason. Indeed this saying, which can mean 'take time to work carefully' or 'take things easy', might be taken as the motto of the trade, as it gives the spirit of the master who was proud of his craft as well as that of the carefree, wandering journeyman.

The Word of Power

Some years ago, in the big kitchen of a County Limerick farmhouse, I was listening to the conversation of two medical students arguing, after the manner of their kind, about symptoms, prognoses and treatments. They were harping upon the theme of the uncertain effect of oral therapy when they were astonished at the remark of an elderly labourer who said 'Ah, sure, the herb is no good at all unless the doctor knows the right verse to go with it.' This patent belief in the word of power, the charm or formula which could work wonders when properly recited, was so new and so surprising to the young medical men that they went off to consult the local doctor, a wise old gentleman who had given forty years of his life in tending the sick of a rural parish. Yes, he told them, many of the old people really believed in the power of the charm. It was all very well to prescribe simple, logical treatment to the average person, but one of the old-timers thought a great deal more of the prescription scrawled in a curious fashion which only the chemist in the local town could understand, for here was the proper ingredient of mystery and secret knowledge. A simple explanation of their ailment, he told us, was unwelcome to such people, and the muttered Latin phrase or high-sounding medical term was absolutely necessary to reassure them that they were in good hands and that the doctor really knew his business.

This belief in the power of charms is as old as humanity and is still found in every corner of the world, so we need not be surprised that it was widely known in Ireland too. There was, of course, an accompanying sense of right and wrong. It was right, people thought (in spite of centuries of Christian teaching) to make use of charms if the desired result was a good one, the healing of illness, the alleviation of pain, the overcoming of a difficulty, but it was quite wrong and reprehensible to make use of charms for an evil purpose, such as to injure somebody or to steal from him. If the charm was not recited absolutely word-perfectly and the right number of times under the right circumstances it could have no effect. And some charms could be recited only by certain people, or were regarded as the exclusive property of certain individuals or families. Sometimes the charm was not only spoken but also written on a piece of paper to be carried about the person; occasionally it was not spoken at all, but merely written down. This writing of charms also was the prerogative of certain people.

Toothache was a dreaded but all too common affliction in the days before proper dental care was known, and the remedy, rough extraction by the local blacksmith or handyman, was at least as painful as the toothache itself. It is hard to blame the unfortunate sufferer who tried to relieve his agony by a little harmless magic, and one of the best known and most widespread charms is one against toothache. The following verse must be said three times without a mistake and with deep concentration: –

> 'As Peter sat on a marble stone
> The Lord came to him all alone.
> 'Oh Peter, Peter, why dost thou shake?'
> 'Oh, Lord, it is my tooth doth ache.'
> The Lord said 'take this for My sake
> And never more your tooth will ache.''

This was believed to be infallible. It is probable that the mental concentration and the full belief in the power of the charm helped to relieve the pain; in matters of this kind we may never leave the psychological effect out of consideration. Here we are reminded of the story of the poor fellow with a toothache who begged a reputed 'wise woman' to charm it away. She wrote some words on a scrap of paper and told him to carry it in his pocket, and deliberately omitted the usual caution that nobody might read the charm. Sure enough the toothache vanished, and the erstwhile sufferer, now aching with curiosity as to what might be the secret of the power, took out the piece of paper and read the words: 'Toothache, fare well till we meet in Hell!' and not only did his peace of mind vanish for many a long day but the toothache returned with increased virulence.

Many of the charms have a story to explain their origin. A tale from West Kerry tells how the Child Jesus and His Mother, fleeing from Herod's soldiers, asked for a night's shelter at a farmer's house. The farmer was a kind, meek little man and welcomed them in, but his wife, an ill-tempered virago, ordered them out of the kitchen and said they could sleep in the barn. Not long afterwards she was smitten with a dreadful pain in her side, and the neighbours, running in at her screams, noticed light shining around the head of the poor Child in the barn, and knowing by this sign that He was a holy person, begged Him to cure the woman, which He did. Ever since then, the following words will banish the pains of gripe: —

Fear ciúin agus bean bhorb
A chuir Iosa in a luí sa cholg.
Cúig méara Iosa agus deárna Muire
Chun scaoileadh agus scaipeadh do chur ar an ngreim,
In ainm an Athar agus an Mhic agus an Spirid Naoimh,
Amen.'

From the form of these charms and the stories which went with them it is easy to see how they became so widespread and popular. They looked like prayers; indeed, many of them were little different from traditional prayers well known in the countryside. Older charms were, without any doubt, well known in the days before Christianity came, but these, to ordinary people, were clearly Christian, and the accompanying stories were proof that Our Lord and the saints had used them. What could be wrong with them, when they were used for a good purpose? Surely the Church's condemnation of charms and magic could not apply to these? This kind of muddled thinking could, and no doubt did, easily lead simple people to overlook the difference between the prayer, with its acceptance of God's will and its appeal to God's goodness, and the charm, which was believed to be powerful in itself. The toothache charm of Peter on the Marble Stone is found in Latin manuscripts of the Middle Ages as well as in the languages of many countries of Europe. It crossed the Atlantic with pioneers and emigrants and still turns up in the New World. Many other charms of similar quasi-religious form are equally widespread.

Other charms there are which have no apparent religious content. Many of us remember the charm for removing warts. If you come by accident on a stone which has a hollow containing water, you should dip your finger in the water, rub it to the warts and say a verse which went like this:

> 'Water in the stone,
> Not to find you here I come,
> But since I met you here today
> I hope you'll take my warts away!'

and, behold! within a week the warts were gone. But even in this simple, and indeed harmless, childish magic there probably is some religious element, from its similarity to the stone fonts of holy water in the porch of the church.

Lower down in the scale there are still other charms which have no religious air about them, and always were regarded as slightly on the wrong side. Once I saw a man working *snadhm na péiste* over the back of a sick calf; he tied a complicated knot in a piece of string and then pulled it free with a jerk, muttering some words at the same time. The symbolism was quite clear, the sickness which had knotted the calf's internal organs must loose like the knot on the string at the word of power. I tried again and again to find out what were the words spoken, but never succeeded; one man told me that they were not right words, that there was no mention of anything holy in them and that he was afraid that there was something of the power of the devil in them. Another charm which is very difficult to discover is *ortha an fhaobhair*, the formula which, when recited, enabled a mower to set an especially sharp and lasting edge on his scythe or reaping hook; here again there was the feeling that evil powers of some kind were invoked. Still worse were the charms which brought success in gambling, or gave the gambler the power to know what his opponent held or to 'colour the cards', that is to change the face of his cards at will; this power could be obtained by holding up an ace of hearts during the solemn part of the Mass, invoking the devil at the same time. People spoke in hushed tones of these patently evil charms, and the general feeling was that it was better to be the victim than the worker of them; even those who knew the words would not reveal them, for fear that harm might come of it.

But there was no reluctance to disclose the 'good' charms. There was *ortha na fola*, said to stop bleeding, which translates like this: 'A child born in Bethlehem was baptised in the river Jordan. The water was so deep and muddy, the child so good and kind. The child said 'Stand, water, stand! Go, blood, go! In the name of the Father and the Son and the Holy Ghost, amen.' Another was *ortha an tromluí*, powerful against nightmares: 'Anne, the mother of Mary, and Mary, the Mother of Jesus, and Elisabeth, the mother of John the Baptist. These three between me and the nightmare from tonight until a year from tonight and tonight itself. In the name of the Father and the Son and the Holy Ghost, Amen.' A person who had difficulty in breathing might be relieved by *ortha an tachtaidh:* 'Seven of the prayers of the Son of God. And seven of the prayers of the two holy women and the angel. And the creed in honour of holy Brighid. O Brighid, come to the help of this poor person!' At these last words the person saying the charm breathed into the mouth of the sufferer and then said seven Paters, seven Aves and the Credo.

Some forty years ago a poor little tradesman came with his troubles to the schoolmaster in a County Limerick village. A local business concern was rebuilding its premises, and he was afraid that the light would be cut off from his little workshop by his big neighbour. What was he to do? The master, as usual, was ready for the occasion; he procured the lid of a plywood tea-chest and a pot of black paint and wrote these two words in bold letters – ANCIENT LIGHTS. 'Hang that in your window where everyone can see it, and something might happen' said the master. The tradesman did so, and sure enough, the very next day certain important persons connected with the new building were seen to examine the notice closely. And they built the high part where it did not cut off the light. But the poor little man went through the rest of his life convinced that this was a powerful charm, and his respect for the master knew no bounds. But can we afford to laugh at him in his simplicity? Is belief in the word of power only to be found among simple people in far away places? Or is some trace of it left in the political catchcry, the pseudo-scientific formula, the name of the mysterious ingredient in the soap powder, the lubricating oil and the patent medicine?

The Basket Maker

The poet who wrote about meeting his love down by the sally gardens expressed himself, perhaps, more euphoniously, but certainly no more romantically, than his fellow bard who sang of a similar encounter in the garden where the praties grow, for in former times and up to fairly recently the sally garden was as humdrum a part of rural economy as the potato field. It was the source of raw material for basket work of all the finer kinds, for which the wild thickets did not provide suitable rods. Basket makers used different kinds of rods for different kinds of work, but osiers were the usual crop in the 'sally gardens' or osieries, which were planted and cultivated with care. The ground was prepared, usually in a damp place, often along a stream or on an island in a river, and the osiers were propagated by cuttings which were, for the most part, set in the ground in bunches of three to give a thick clump; the soil had been fertilised with lime or whatever manure local custom demanded, and some owners spread more fertiliser during growth. In two or three years the twigs were ready to be cut for the basketmaker's use. Some osieries were small, a quarter-acre or so, but some were as much as ten or more acres in extent, and the rent paid for the sally garden was as much as that for potato land. Many of them belonged to local basket makers for their own supply, but we learn that in County Meath a hundred and fifty years ago there were many acres of osiers grown for sale to the Dublin basket makers, who were ready to pay ten pounds an acre and cut the rods themselves. Many farmers grew them as a crop, and sold them at fair and market, or by arrangement to the local basketmakers, for about two shillings a hundred. Incidentally the 'hundred' was made up of 40 'hands' of three rods each, with a 'tilly' of eight rods, that is, 128 rods.

In these days of readymade containers of plastics, card, sheet-metal and many other materials, it is hard for us to imagine how important containers of basketwork were in former times, for storage and for carrying. The farmer's wife took eggs to market in a basket, her little daughter carried her school books in another. There were baskets for fish and turf, for ore and potatoes, for seaweed, bread and glassware and a hundred other products; the 'kish of brogues' is proverbial. There was no parish without its basketmaker, and many parishes had employment for four or five, besides which many a handyman made his own.

Some basketmakers confined themselves to making the larger and coarser kinds. There was the hurdle-maker; a hurdle, as we know, is a large sheet of wickerwork, of any required shape or size. Occasionally we see them yet in use as shelters for tender growing plants, but formerly they were used as fences, to reinforce floors and repair roads. The builder found numerous uses for them; the vaulted roofs of many of our old castles were supported by wickerwork forms when being built, the imprint of the rods is still frequently to be seen in the old mortar. They were used as scaffolding or framing for walls, bridges, dams and many other constructions. They were used, too, for building material; our old literature has many accounts of people living in wattle huts, and archaeologists in their excavations find the footings of walls made of wickerwork. Indeed, there is no need to go back to the distant past to find this. There are many old houses still standing which have internal partition walls or parts of walls made of clay-plastered wickerwork; chimney funnels of this material were quite common, as were walls in which the wattle was not woven rods but straw or hay rope woven on a wooden frame. Sometimes these partition walls were not plastered. An English visitor to a County Kildare farmhouse in the 1690s tells of a room cut off by a partition of plastered wattle, but with a wattled door 'which was not impervious to Argus eyes, and made rather to keep out the swine or the calves that for either any privacy or warmth'. In west County Limerick there still is a memory of partitions which were made of wickerwork of smooth peeled rods which had been dyed and then woven to show bands of different colours; naturally such a work of art would not be plastered over.

A worthy parson, a certain Reverend Mr. James Hall, who seems to have spent much of his time in travelling, visited Ireland in the first decade of the last century, and reported from County Limerick: 'As I had done in the county of Kerry, and elsewhere, I found, in the county of Limerick, the common people extremely fond of wickerwork. Their doors with padlocks, windows, cradles, beds, chairs, &c, &c. are, in general, all of wicker-work. In one house I observed a bed of extremely neat wicker-work, sufficient to contain two grown people, shaped like a cradle; the head jutting out as if it had been one.' This is borne out by the more recent tradition of those parts, which tells of chairs, stools and cradles as well as doors and window shutters made like this in our grandfathers' day. And, lest anyone should imagine that a basketwork door is little protection, against the wind, we are also told by the old people that there were expert makers of straw-rope mats which were so tightly woven as to keep out any draught; these mats were hung inside the wicker doors.

The basket maker's tools were few and simple. He had a short-handled billhook and a sharp knife to cut the rods, a couple of instruments like thick awls for poking the rods apart when another rod was to be put in while making the basket and another tool, like a very blunt chisel, for pushing them together again. The good basket-maker liked to cut and prepare his own rods. They were cut in the autumn, after the leaves had fallen, and were left for several weeks to season. Then, for fine work, the bark was taken off by soaking the rods in hot water (some just put them in a pool of a stream for a time) and rubbing the loosened bark off. This left the rods a beautiful pale gold colour, and some craftsmen improved this by dyeing the rods different colours and using the coloured rods to make patterns in the work; well-dyed rods held the colour for years.

In our part of the country the principal kinds of baskets were those used in house and farm. There was the egg-basket, while was oval in shape, up to two feet long and eighteen inches wide, curved in towards the bottom but flat underneath so that it would stand; the lid was an oval sheet of basketwork, about half an inch larger than the basket top all round, and with a long slot running across it, through which the strong handle stuck up when the basket was covered. The child's 'school-basket' was a different shape, rectangular in section but tapering slightly towards the bottom, about a foot by nine inches on top and eight or nine inches high, with a hinged lid.

There were two small openings on the outer edge of the lid and two loops on the front of the basket went through these when the lid was closed, and a small stick secured it; the handle was a wicker loop fastened to the middle of the lid. Then there was the *sciath*, like a large oval dish with a rounded bottom, used for carrying turf, potatoes and so on – it had a strong handle on each side, and was particularly apt for potatoes as these could be washed and drained in it.

Formerly back-baskets and panniers for pack-saddles were used, but these had disappeared by our time, although the old people still remembered them in use. Their main function was to bring turf out of the bog as soon as it was dry, so as to stack it on the roadside where it could be loaded into carts, but we heard of their use, on both man and beast, for carrying manure into the tillage fields; some of these, especially those used on horses or donkeys, had bottoms hinged like a door so that the contents could fall out when the securing pin was pulled and so save the trouble of taking the basket off the shoulders or pack-saddle. In former times, and, indeed, until recently in rough country, these back-baskets and panniers were the normal means of transport for all sorts of goods. Like the *sciath*, and unlike the finer forms of baskets they were made from unpeeled rods, often of the coarser hazel or the black sally instead of the fine white sally, as we called the osier.

Another form of basket much used in former times and still to be found in a few areas is circular with a flat bottom and a rim which stands perpendicularly and is about two to three inches high, some small, a foot or so in diameter, others as much as three feet across. These had the important function of keeping food hot in cold weather; the basket was laid on top of a large pot and the boiled potatoes carefully strained through it so that the hot water was caught in the pot supporting the basket, and so the potatoes were kept warm. Plates containing the bacon or fish to be eaten with the potatoes were laid on the basket too, and the diners sat around and helped themselves. These baskets were well made of peeled rods and always washed after use; one or more of them might be seen hanging up to dry on the sunny side of many a house in Connaught and west Ulster up to quite recently.

A curious feature of some of the Irish baskets of larger size, such as the back-baskets and panniers, was the method of making. Normally a basket maker begins by forming the bottom of the basket and then continuing up the sides and finishing with the rim, but in the big Irish baskets the rim was made first, by sticking into the ground in the shape of the basket rim a number of strong rods which were to be the uprights of the basket and then weaving the other rods through them, finishing with the bottom. This appears to be a very ancient method of working, and has the great advantage of holding the work quite firm, which is especially necessary in a big job such as the making of a 'kish'. Nowadays when such a load as turf or live pigs is carried on a horse cart, a 'creel' or 'rail', that is a strong detachable lattice of wood, is used, but formerly this function was performed, especially in the 'low-backed cars', by the 'kish', a large basket fitting the floor of the cart and made of very strong rods. We are told that good kish rods cost 2s. a hundred in 1802 and that it took about two hundred rods and a day's work to make one, for which the basket maker got four or five shillings, which does not seem to leave him much profit unless he grew his own rods. Turf was sold by the kish in the Dublin market; the kish was supposed to hold a cubic yard and to contain 215 sods of dry turf.

A list of all the products of the basket makers art would include, besides the types of basket mentioned above, many other forms of basket and hamper as well as chairs, stools and cradles, calf-muzzles, fish and bird traps, doors and hurdles, strainers and sieves, protective coverings for bottles and other fragile objects, forms for dressmakers and wigmakers and the bodywork of gigs and phaetons. In ancient times a common form of boat was of basket-work covered with the hide of a horse or cow, a form which survived until recently in the Boyne coracle and in some older forms of the currach of the west coast. Soldiers used wickerwork in fortifications much as sandbags are used today, notably a device called a gabion, which was a big cylindrical basket open at both ends; a row of these stood upright on the ground and when filled with earth made a stout barricade. Even the humble *sciath* which carried turf or potatoes seems to have a respectable ancestry, for *sciath* means a shield, and the name may be a direct memory of the use of wicker shields by warriors of old.

The Cooper

That hideous adjunct to any of our towns, the rubbish dump, is usually in some spot removed from the public gaze, but those who come upon it will notice that, of all the cast-off objects and fragments there to be seen, none are more numerous than containers of all sorts, from sardine tins to road-oil drums and from paper bags to broken bottles. This is the age of the 'individual wrapper', when everything comes in its own packet, whether it is a bar of chocolate or a refrigerator. There are glass bottles and jars by the million, envelopes, packets and boxes of paper and cardboard, tin-cans and metal cases of all shapes and sizes, and an enormous and ever-growing variety of plastic holders. And yet many of us remember the time so recently gone when the little country shops purchased their goods in bulk and weighed them out to the customers, when old newspapers were commonly used as wrapping material and the school children swopped their discarded copybooks for a few sweets so that the shopkeeper could use the leaves for the small twists we called *tóisíns*. I recall the indignation of one small boy whose granny gave him a present of sweets when he found that the *tóisín* was a page from one of his own copybooks on which all the sums were wrong – with the master's comments in puce pencil. The notion of having everything neatly made up in tin or packet or bottle is quite recent, and the commonest type of strong container in which the shopkeeper got his wares was the barrel.

We remember the half-dozen barrels arranged on one side of the grocer's shop, one with red herrings, a second with pigs' heads, another with apples, and so on. Table ware and lamp glasses came to the hardware shop in barrels, as well as turpentine, putty and all manner of oils. In our grandfathers' day barrels were used even more widely; fruit and biscuits came in small barrels, tar and paraffin in big ones. Anybody who wanted a barrel of any size had only to go to the shop and ask for one. He might get it for nothing, or if he had to pay it cost only a shilling or two. The barrels which had held oil or tar made good water butts, and other barrels of all sizes were most useful about the house and farm. Most houses had a clean barrel for salting the bacon when the pig was killed. A broken tar-barrel made a fierce and ready fuel and on festive occasions an empty one made a splendid bonfire. Sometimes they were put to more sinister uses. Mary Leadbeater, the Quaker lady of Ballitore who left such a vivid account of the Rising of 1798, tells with horror how she heard one of the Government supporters, 'a fat tobacconist from Carlow', boasting of how he had helped to burn an unfortunate croppy alive in a tar-barrel.

Besides the barrels, every house in town as well as in the country had its complement of tubs, some formed from cut-down casks, others specially made. The milk was set for skimming in shallow keelers, the butter was made in dash or barrel churn and packed in firkins. The table ware was washed in a small tub, the clothes in a larger one and a very big one held the newly woven woollen cloth and blankets for cleansing and fulling. One of the high moments in the life of any small country boy was when he launched out for distant lands in his mother's washtub in the stream at the bottom of the meadow. A big keeler made a fine pond to sail toy boats in, and came in handy for apple bobbing on Hallow E'en. The children were washed in a tub in front of the kitchen fire, and before the coming of the modern bath-tub adults usually bathed themselves in a big barrel.

All these numerous forms of barrel, keg and tub were made by the cooper. There was hardly a village or a parish in the whole country without one of these crafts-men hard at work, either for local orders or for sale on the market day when he spread out a selection of his wares on the street and did a brisk trade with the farmers and their wives. But the main strength of the craft was in the seaport towns, especially those on the south coast where the provision trade was of great importance. When Arthur Young visited Cork in 1776 he found 700 coopers at work in that town, making casks for the ex-port of salted beef and bacon. In an average year at that period the port of Cork sent out more than 100,000 casks of meat of various kinds, mostly beef and pork much of which went to provision the British navy, and very nearly the same number of firkins of butter. At Water-ford, a smaller port, an average year's export might amount to half of that of Cork, while similar quantities were handled at Dublin, Limerick and other ports. Bel-fast had 115 coopers at work in 1791. In the long voy-ages of the sailing ships, large amounts of fresh water had to be carried, and the great water-casks meant more work for the cooper. Every ship of any size had a cooper among the crew to attend to the water and provision casks and make new ones when required. The fishing ports made great demands on the trade. Almost all kinds of fish, salted, smoked or dried, were packed in barrels. And every distillery and brewery in the country had its own team of coopers constantly at work.

Coopering is an expert craft. A well made barrel is probably the strongest as well as the safest form of wooden container; it will stand a great deal of rough handling and can scarcely be broken apart with any tool less than a sledgehammer. Even such tricky substances as chemicals and gunpowder were safely conveyed in bar-rels; often these were double casks, one inside the other with packing between – the tragic explosion on the Dub-lin quay in 1597, when a load of six tons of powder for Queen Elizabeth's army blew up and killed nearly 200 people, was caused by the powder having been sent from England in single casks, and no doubt some master-cooper found himself in trouble over this. Luckily such happenings were rare.

The cooper had a set of implements peculiar to his craft. First there were axes, cleavers and adzes of various shapes with which the staves were roughed out. Recently a murderous looking tool was exposed at a local exhibition as an ancient battle-axe; it was, in fact, a cooper's axe the use of which had been forgotten in the district. Then there were planes and shaves of curved shape for the finishing of the staves; this was the real secret of the cooper's craft, for the barrel was as good – or as bad – as the staves in it. Every line in the stave was curved or angled. It was wider in the middle than at the ends and smoothly curved from end to end; it was curved from side to side too, convex on the outside and concave on the inside; each edge had to have the angle of the radius of the barrel so that when fitted together they were absolutely flush. All this needed exact measurements and an expert eye and hand in the cutting and shaping as well as in the bending which was done by heating or steaming the wood. At some stages of the shaping the stave was held in a 'mare'; this was a sort of stool on one end of which the cooper sat, while at the other end there was a large wooden clamp operated by his feet to hold the work firmly and leave both hands free for the tools.

The barrel is held together by hoops and the cooper had to be an expert in measuring and making these. In casks used for dry materials these were often of wood, but casks to hold liquids had iron hoops. At the first setting up of the staves, the 'raising of the barrel' as the cooper called it, the staves were held in a 'raising hoop' of standard size for the particular type of barrel and two or three other iron hoops were put on so that one end of the barrel was shaped. (The hoops used here were wider and stronger than ordinary hoops; they were replaced by ordinary hoops at a later stage and used over and over again in the making of further barrels). The half shaped barrel was then heated or steamed in the smaller workshops by being held over a cresset in which a fire was lit. This softened the staves and they were drawn together at the other end and secured by hoops. Then the shaping hoops were taken off and ordinary hoops put on at the other end. Now the cooper had a barrel open at both ends, and the next operation was the fitting of a disc of wood over each opening. For small kegs this might be a circle cut from one piece of wood, but more usually it was made up of several pieces usually dowelled together. A certain amount of work had to be done on the ends of the staves before the head was fitted. They were pared even all around and a bevel cut all around the inner edge. Then the inside surface at each end was smoothed with a special curved plane and another plane-like tool, called a 'croze' was used to cut a slot all around the inside about two inches below the stave ends. At this time too, the bung hole through which the liquid could be filled into the finished barrel was cut with a brace and smoothed; good quality barrels and those meant for repeated use – such as beer kegs – had a metal ring fitted into the bung hole. The cooper then loosened or removed the last hoop at each end and pushed the 'heads' – the circular wooden ends – into position; this required some expert work in pushing the second 'head' into its slot by means of a long tool operated through the bung hole. Often some packing material was used to make the joints perfectly watertight; country coopers used partly peeled rushes for this. Then any rough spots on the outer surface of the barrel were smoothed off with a plane or a shave.

The finished barrel was tested for leaks by being filled with boiling water, and if any leak was found the hoops were tightened still further or minor repairs were done with small pieces of wood. Barrels intended for dry substances, such as apples or soda, did not have to be wateright; it was sufficient if they were strong enough for their job. They were headed at one end only and the other head was supplied separately, to be put in when the barrel had been filled. In most cases the heads of 'dry' barrels were not fitted into a slot. Instead a wooden hoop was nailed around inside, the head was laid upon this and another wooden hoop nailed on over it to hold it firmly. The removal of the outer wooden hoop permitted the head to be taken off so as to get at the goods in the barrel. Semi-dry merchandise, such as herrings in pickle, needed a slotted head, and in their barrels the head was put in and taken out by moving the last hoops.

For dry barrels almost any sound wood was suitable, but barrels to hold liquids were usually made of oak. In former times, when oak woods flourished in Ireland and there was a great export of Irish timber, there was more than sufficient to supply the Irish coopers and leave huge quantities of barrel staves over for export. The wine merchants of France and Spain were eager buyers of Irish 'pipe-staves' as they were called; Sir Walter Raleigh, who dabbled much in Irish affairs, obtained a permit from Queen Elizabeth to export barrel-staves and for several years sent off about a quarter of a million staves each year, clearing whole forests of fine oak trees in the process. When the Irish woods were thus wasted without replanting, and a timber famine set in, the trade was reversed, and huge quantities of oak and other timbers were imported to supply the coopers in the hey-day of the provision trade. For the most part this came in rough pieces of suitable size for splitting into staves.

In a big centre like Cork a cooper might spend all his days making one type of barrel. In other places, especially in the countryside, the cooper did much more varied work, making not only barrels, tubs, buckets and churns for general use, but also fine work like staved piggins to be used as drinking vessels, small kegs with brass hoops and taps to hold whiskey or wine on the table of the 'big house', brass-hooped tubs to hold plates and dishes, or bread and biscuits, or turf beside the parlour fire.

The coopers' last strongholds were the breweries and the distilleries, but here too, especially in the breweries, the wooden casks are yielding to metal containers, and the specialised cooper is going the way of his country cousin, into the obscurity that has swallowed so many other skilled craftsmen.

The Master

Of all the familiar figures of the Irish countryside in the last century none, probably, left more of an impression on the community than the 'masther', the local school teacher, the guide, philosopher and friend of the whole parish. A hundred years or so ago, a large number, sometimes as many as half, of the inhabitants of most country parts were illiterate and even those who had acquaintance with the printed page and the quill pen were lost when it came to anything more advanced than ordinary reading and writing. Thus the master's store of knowledge, small though it may have been from the viewpoint of modern scholarship, was highly respected and much valued by his neighbours, nor did they hesitate to draw upon it when the necessity arose. For the master, although set above them by his erudition, was none the less one of themselves. The priest and the doctor were, of course, ever ready to attend to the ills of soul and body, and each of them was highly respected, but they were usually strangers to the immediate locality, appointed by some distant authority, while the master was, most often, a local man, one whose people were known to all. Again, nobody in his right senses would expect the priest or the doctor to draw up a will or an indenture, or survey a bit of conacre or arbitrate in the division of seventeen irregular wynds of hay among three partners who had bought 2 acres, 3 roods and 1 perch of meadowing. Such matters, however, were among the most minor of the requests the fulfilling of which occupied a great part of the master's spare time. And while there was a certain material advantage to the master in all this, such as the goose at Christmas or the occasional load of turf, he was seldom moved by mercenary motives in his help to the public and was just as ready to write a document for the poor cottier in return for a blessing as he was to draw a will for a rich farmer who would be sure to show his thanks in a more worldly fashion.

The same held for the dispensation of learning. When the regular school was over and evening had come, there was often a group of boys and girls getting extra teaching at the master's house, for often he was a competent classical scholar and could lead aspirants to the clerical college or the university into the mysteries of Latin and Greek, while such subjects as book-keeping and business methods were in demand by budding clerks and shop assistants. Those who could afford it – as the farmers could – paid the master a fee for this teaching, but the poor man's son was not turned away because the ready cash was not to hand. Even today there are many men in high position who owe their start in life to some quiet bespectacled old gentleman, long since dead, who conned Horace and Homer with them by the light of an oil lamp winter night after winter night. Many and complicated were the confabulations between the master and the anxious parents who were at a loss to know to what trade or profession they should put young Johnny, and sometimes it happened that the master used his prestige and position as intellectual and moral bludgeons to force some grasping parent to give a bright boy or girl the extra couple of years of schooling that might lead to higher things instead of putting them to work on the land or domestic service. Success here brought the master a glow of pride, and in his declining years the Christmas post brought reminders of his success, the letters from many parts of the world, the book from an American bishop, the fountain pen from the mayor of a great Australian city, the lovely painting on silk from a Mother Abbess in China. But much more difficult and much less rewarding was his task when he had to convince some doting mother that young Mickey (known to the seven parishes as being as thick as the proverbial ditch) was not, in spite of the broad acres and the big bank account, exactly the stuff of which prelates, professors and judges are made.

The master drew up wills and diplomatically avoided all invitations to decide who should get the inheritance. He wrote all sorts of papers and sometimes guided the hand that signed 'X (his mark)' at the bottom. He prepared articles of apprenticeship for boys who wished to learn a trade; one parent on perusing one of these was gravely perturbed at its simplicity – not a 'whereas' or a 'herinafter' or a 'party of the second part' to be seen in it! But the master, as ever, rose to the occasion, and an old historical tome yielded the text of a fearsome document much in demand in Medieval trade guilds, which stretched interminably into subordinate clauses, provided for all manner of improbable contingencies and bristled with admonitions and prohibitions calculated to curl the hair on an apprentice's head and whiten that of the tradesman to whose care he was committed. In this case the master's little joke rebounded on his own head, for the fame of this noble indenture spread far and wide and thereafter none of his clients was satisfied with anything less.

The master was an expert in land surveying, and the surveyors' chain was a familiar part of his equipment. Often he had two chains, one for statute measure and one for plantation measure, and was able to convert 'Irish acres' to 'English acres' in his head. One old man, who was appointed to one of the new National Schools in the 1860s, used to recall with a wry smile that his surveying and accounting for a rich but unlettered farmer for several years brought him a fee of once and a half times as much as his salary for the long hours spent in teaching, although his help to the farmer never took up more than an hour of his evening and usually much less.

Sometimes inordinate demands were made on the master's good offices, as when he was asked to mediate between bitterly quarrelling neighbours or to act as a matchmaker or to speak up in court or to the landlord for some tongue-tied rustic. An extreme case of this occurred to the master who was cycling along a West Limerick road to his school on a summer morning sixty years ago when he was stopped by the elderly widow of a strong farmer.

'In the honour of God, Masther, will you come in and bate Johnny for me? 'Tis how he won't get up out of bed for me in spite of my best!'

'Now, Mrs. Mullarkey, don't you think that a more moderate approach to the problem might be advisable?'

'Yerra, *Grá Dé ináirde*, Masther, you needn't be one sign in dread of him! Haven't I him tied down to the bed with the hay-rope, and he sleeping like a rock of bogdeal, and the handle of the brush ready and all for you to give under him? And, God help us all, Master (sob!), sure I'd bate him myself, only I haven't the strength!'

The bold Johnny, incidentally, was a young giant of twenty-eight, six feet two in height and as broad as a door, his lapse on this occasion being caused by an all-night party to which he had gone unknown to the old woman. But the master had at least to speak to Johnny, and the two men had a good laugh over the incident when they got the mother out of the room.

The master was much in demand on all social occasions. Not a party, dance or raffle was held to which he was not invited, and, being a diplomatic man, he went to them all. If he could sing or play an instrument he had to entertain the company, but his favourite party piece was the recitation. 'Fontenoy', 'Robert Emmet's speech from the dock', 'Shamus O'Brien', 'The Blacksmith of Limerick' and such pieces were on the tip of his tongue, and if he was anything of a poet, as so many masters were, his own verses delighted his hearers, although often there was more pedantry than poetry in them, as for instance –

'The Universe'

'Each visible or telescopic star that gems the face of the
    sidereal sky,
And sheds its feeble radiance from afar, and each of those
    that optic powers defy
To see them, is a sun around which fly elliptically plan-
    etary spheres,
Which with their lunar satellites enjoy light, heat and
    motion, seasons, days and years.
Oh what divine omnipotence herein appears!

'Then what a vast immensity of space must to each solar
    system be assigned,
Wherein each planet runs its orbic race, uninterfered with
    by its rolling kind.
But by attractive forces which do bind them mutually

and to the solar ball
Round which they roll. If we but bear in mind how
   countless are these systems, we must call
that Wisdom infinite which oversees them all.

'And who, reflecting thus, could ever dare offend the
   Lord whose all-creative will
by but one act all worlds and what they bear called forth,
   arranged and harmonised, and still
directs, conserves and cares. Such thoughts should fill
   all hearts with love and fear of God. May we
All through his holy grace the ends fulfill for which He
   made us, that we yet may see,
love and enjoy Him during all eternity.'

The composer of this poem, one Martin O'Sullivan, had
no education other than that of a hedge-school supple-
mented by his own reading. He taught a hedge-school
himself until appointed to a National School at Athea,
County Limerick. Fame wider than that of a country ped-
agogue and poet was to be his, for his thoughts were
occupied by the distress caused by the potato blight, and
he became convinced that it came from atmospheric elec-
tricity. He sought to remedy this by suspending a net-
work of fine copper wire over a chosen potato bed, and
was so gratified by the result that he plucked up the
courage to communicate his experiment to the agricultural big-wigs in Dublin, who duly tried it out and sent
word of it to their foreign colleagues, and soon the humble
village master in County Limerick was in lengthy cor-
respondence with savants in many seats of learning from
Chicago to St. Petersburg. His theory and an account of
his experiments may still be read by the curious in his
pamphlet *Electro-Culture of Potatoes*.

Few masters spread their fame so wide as did Martin
O'Sullivan. Most of them were content to teach their little
schools and be friends to all the countryside, respected
by gentle and simple alike. In places remote from schools
of the more advanced kind even the sons of the parson
and the landlord might sit at the feet of the local master,

and Protestant and Catholic alike were taught fairly by him. Of course, at a time when the teaching of a simple historical truth might – if the said truth was unpalatable to the government – be twisted into a treasonable utterance, the master was often accused of 'sedition' and was sometimes deep in the councils of the underground liberation movements. Once, in the early part of the last century, the master of Castlemahon was accused by the local tyrant of having taken part in a Whiteboy raid on a mail coach, but proved his innocence by the presence of the landlord's son, a youth preparing to enter Trinity College, Dublin, at his Latin class on the night in question. This master's grandson, an aged man in the 1920s – still recalled his grandfather's lifelong bitterness because the tyrant had seized his shelf of manuscript books in his zeal for the discovery of 'treasonable documents' and, finding them to be no more than anthologies of Gaelic, English, Latin and Greek literary pieces, historical and geographical extracts and a teacher's miscellaneous notes on all sorts of learned questions, threw them on the fire in disgust. Such books, carefully written in elegant copperplate by the light of many a midnight candle and carefully bound in boards and leather – for bookbinding was one of the master's hereditary skills – formed the stock-in-trade of many a rural scholar. Few of these books have survived, but those that have should be preserved as precious relics of the 'masthers' who loved learning and did so much to raise up their fellow men in days that were bitter and dark.

Our Family Names

There are many parishes in Ireland in which every second house is occupied by people of the same surname, Ryans, Flahertys, Smiths, O'Dohertys or whatever the predominant local name may be. You may find ten Eugene O'Sullivans or Michael Byrnes or Patrick Kellys living close together. There must be some method of distinguishing between individuals, so that when you are speaking about Nicholas Walsh your hearers will know that you mean the Nicholas who has the farm with the grass of twenty five cows in Derreen, and not Nicholas from Ballybeg or Nicholas the shopkeeper or young Nicholas who is away at school. Some kind of extra name is needed for identification, and Irish people, especially Irish country people, are expert at supplying these names. Often it is by adding the name of the place where the family lives. One family of Ryans, among many in the district, lives in Derrymore, so they are called Ryan of Derrymore, or Ryan Derrymore. Then they may easily become just Derrymore — 'I met one of the Derrymores today'. And one of them might be known generally as John Derrymore. Or it might be their occupation which distinguishes them. John Ryan the harness maker is generally called 'The Saddler' and his family 'the Saddlers', the children being 'Johnny the Saddler', 'Mickey the Saddler' and 'Mary the Saddler'. Denis O'Shaughnessy is 'Dinny the Smith', Michael Farrell is 'Mickey the Fiddler', Ann Murphy is 'Hannie the Weaver', all from the occupation of the father or the grandfather. A prevailing hair colour may supply the name; you have Ryan Bán, Ryan Ruadh, Ryan Dubh, Ryan Liath. The most common kind of supplementary name, however, comes from the father's name. John Ryan is commonly called Jack. His son Michael is known as Mickey Jack. Time goes on and Michael's family are called the Mickey Jacks; there is Paddy Mickey Jack and Willie Mickey Jack and Molly Mickey Jack. Usually it stops at three steps. Patrick Ryan's son, in this family, will probably be called Michael Paddy Mickey, although some people will go the whole way and say Michael Paddy Mickey Jack. And the family, especially if they continue to live in the old place, may carry on the name 'The Jacks' for several generations.

Sometimes it is the mother's name that is given. The classic example of this is, of course, 'Jímín Mháire Thaidhg' in the story, where, as usual, there is a good reason why the mother's rather than the father's name was given to the children. As the hero of the story explains, his mother was boss of the house and his father did not count for much at home, and the neighbours showed their understanding of the situation by giving her name, and not his, to the children. Very often the mother's name was used like this because she was a widow; her husband died while the children were young and so the children were associated, in the neighbours' minds, with her.

As we might expect, many distinguishing names are no more than nicknames, and as we all know, Irish country people are very skilful in the coining of appropriate nicknames which not only describe the person named but also show quite clearly the local opinion of the individual named. Some are flattering, some are just descriptive, some are funny in a friendly sort of way and others spring from a malicious kind of humour, while some are downright insulting. A man might be called 'Whistler' or 'Fiddler' or 'Hurler' because of his prowess in that direction, and the name might be kept on with a certain degree of pride by his descendants. Then you had Long Dan and Brown Jack and Pats Buí, from stature or hair colour, and such names were accepted without complaint. A man might be called 'the Boyo' because he liked to play practical jokes, or 'Parnell' because he looked like Charles Stuart Parnell, and take a certain amount of pride from the fact that he was nicknamed because of an amiable characteristic, but if he was called 'Geannc' because his nose was turned up, or 'the Firkin' because he was small and stout, or 'Bandy' because of the shape of his legs, he might not be so pleased about it, whatever amusement the neighbours might get from the name. And of course the name was passed on to the next generation and the one after that, and while a man might be glad to hear himself named as 'one of the Leaguers' because his grandfather was prominent in the Land League, he would hate to be called 'Bags' in memory of his greatgrandfather who had to take the roads in the Famine years. And we need not stress the meaning of nicknames like 'Mickeen the Bailiff' or 'Dawley the Informer' or 'Neddy the Jumper', especially when they are continued into the fourth or fifth generation.

It often happens that an individual may have several names. On the voters list it appeared as Timothy Ryan. His immediate friends call him Teddy. The neighbours around call him Big Thady. Acquaintances farther away call him Tim Ryan Ballybrack and his family the Ballybracks. And he takes all these as a matter of course. But there is also 'Taidhgín Go Aisy' because of his cautious manner; he does not like to hear that. Worst of all a man with a drop too much taken at a fair might open an old sore by calling him 'Marksman' because his greatgrandfather was tried for shooting a land grabber in the bad old times. There are six names all applied to the same person, and that is by no means unusual.

Names like these come and go. They seldom survive the third generation. But the custom which applies them and the method by which they are given are really the same custom and method which gave permanent surnames to our forefathers. Surnames form one of our strongest links with the past; they tell us from where we came and to what kind of people we belong. They are the shrine of our family pride, the token of our good reputation. And if some of us are a bit proud and boastful about them, can't we point back over the centuries to famous bearers of the same name? Surnames came into use at different periods in different countries. Even yet there are some countries, Iceland for instance, where surnames are not in common use and a man is called directly the son of his father: Jon Magnusson is the son of Magnus Sigurdsson who is the son of Sigurd Sveinsson. But surnames have been in ordinary use in Ireland for close on a thousand years, and they can tell us a lot about our history and our background not only as individuals but as a community and a nation.

The old saying 'By Mac and O you'll always know true Irishmen, they say, but if they lack both O and Mac, no Irishmen are they.' is not quite correct, but is near enough to the truth for our oldest surnames. According to the Irish tradition a surname was a claim of descent from somebody, not just a convenient label. The surname O'Neill comes from Niall Glúndubh, High King of Ire-

land, who died in A.D. 919, and his grandson Donal Ó
Néill is the first O'Neill mentioned in history. But at a
very early stage in the development of surnames we find
other families of O'Neill, like the O'Neills of Thomond,
the O'Neills of the Decies and the O'Neills of Leinster,
and some of them claim a different descent from the O'
Neills of Ulster. We can understand that there were several heroes or famous men with the Christian name Niall,
and so there could be several families of O'Neill quite
unrelated to each other. The commonest Irish surname
is Murphy, which comes from Murchadh, 'Sea-hero'. But
there are two different Irish forms of the name, Ó Murchadha and Mac Murchadha, neither of which represents
descent from one particular sturdy mariner of the past,
as there are several unrelated families bearing the same
form of the name. There was Mac Murchadha (also
spelled Mac Murchaidh) of Tyrone, Mac Murchaidh of
Roscommon and Mac Murchadha of Leinster. The Leinster
family takes the name from Murchadh, King of Leinster,
who was grandfather of no less a personage than Dermot
Mac Murrogh who gave the Normans their excuse for
coming to Ireland. The surname Ó Murchadha was borne
by at least three ancient families, situated in Ulster, in
County Sligo and in County Wexford.

The next most common Irish name is Kelly. But this
hides several Irish names. Ó Ceallaigh (grandson of Ceal-
lach, the 'Warrior') was the name of seven or eight different families, the principal being Ó Ceallaigh of Uí
Máine who held wide lands in Counties Galway and
Roscommon; there were also Ó Ceallaigh of Loughinoso-
lin, County Derry, Ó Ceallaigh of Laoighis, Ó Ceallaigh
Breagh (County Meath), and others of Wicklow, of Sligo
and of west County Cork. Then there were the Mac Ceal-
laighs of County Galway, of County Leitrim and of the
Isle of Man. Other Kellys belong to the Mac Giolla Cheal-
laigh family, claiming descent from King Guaire the
Hospitable of Connaught, although some members of
this stock prefer to spell the name Kilkelly or MacGil-
kelly. There was a Mac Gaochlaoich (Son of the Blind
Hero) family in west County Cork, some of the des-

cendants of which are now called Kelly while others prefer Coakly. And at least two other old names, Ó Cadhla and Ó Caolaidhe, have become confused in places with O'Kelly, although here again there are other spellings, Kiely, Keeley, Quealy, Queely and so on.

Third on the list of Irish surnames is O'Sullivan, and here we are on fairly easy ground. This was a great Tipperary family until they were pushed out by the Norman invasion, when they moved into the south west corner of Ireland to become the most powerful family of that area, with several branches, such as O'Sullivan Beare, O'Sullivan Mór and O'Sullivan Maol, all related to each other in blood. But an old County Cavan and County Longford family, Ó Súileacháin, has many descendants who now write their name O'Sullivan although they have no connexion with the Munster O'Sullivans.

When Norsemen and Danes settled in Ireland about a thousand years ago they had not yet begun to use surnames generally, but according as they became assimilated they took surnames after the Irish fashion, or were given them by their Irish neighbours, by using O or Mac, and these names are not easy to distinguish at first sight from the older Irish ones. We have Doyle, O'Loughlin, Cotter, MacAuliffe, MacKeever and MacGetrick. The first two simply claim descent from a 'Dark Foreigner' and a 'Norseman', and probably were first used by the neighbours of the settlers and then accepted as their own by the ancestors of the families who now bear them. The others show descent from Ottar, Olaf, Ivor and Sitric, names as common among the Norsemen as Donal and Dermot were among the Irish. There are several other names, like Broderick, Harrold, Sugrue (from Broder, Harald, Sigfrid).

The fourth most common surname in Ireland is Walsh, which, of course, means a Welshman. The Normans invaded Ireland from Wales, the leaders mostly Welsh-Normans and the soldiers and settlers to a large extent native Welshmen. Here again we can take it that the surname was given by the neighbours, and accepted by the Walshes. Two other forms of this name are Brannock, from the Irish *Breathnach*, and Wallace, from the Norman-French *de Walys*, both meaning Welshman. Of course there were, from the first settlement, many different families of Walshes quite unrelated to each other.

The fifth most common Irish surname is Smith, a name found all over Ireland but very numerous in Counties Louth, Meath and Cavan. It belongs to many different families. In older times the blacksmith was a much more important man than he is to day, not just a shoer of horses and a mender of broken gates and pitchforks, but the maker of nearly all weapons, tools, instruments and utensils. He was held in very high estimation in ancient Ireland; the master smith could dine with the king and his doctors, chiefs, bards and judges. It is quite natural that it became a surname, as it did in other countries too. In Ireland we had Mac Gabhann and Ó Gabhann, notable families in Clare and Cavan, but descendants of notable smiths in all parts of the country were given the name, and, just to complicate things, many people from Britain bearing the name Smith (Smyth, Smythe) settled here and there in Ireland. Indeed there are not many 'trade-names' of old Irish origin; we have O'Hickey (descendant of the healer), Mac an Bháird (of the Poet), Mac an tSaoir (of the Craftsman), Mac Inerny (of the Church Steward), MacEntee (of the scholar) and a few others, against the very large number of English trade names in our midst, Baker, Butcher, Hunter, Archer, Fletcher (arrowmaker), Fisher, Millar, Slater, Thatcher, Butler, Taylor, Wright and many others. In the same way, there are not many old Irish names taken directly from places, hair colour, characteristics and dispositions, while there are very many such names among the Normans and the Palesmen, like Brown, Green and White, Petty, Little, Curtis, Savage, Fox, Wren, Field, Woods, Church, London, Bolton, East and West.

The Normans gave us Fitzgerald and the other Fitznames, as well as other surnames now very widespread in Ireland; just to name a few we have Barry, Bourke, Cogan, Dalton, Lacy, Hussey, Keating, Power, Nugent, Prendergast, Purcell, Roche, Palmer, Plunkett, Butler, Tyrrell, White and Woulfe. Some parts of the country are studded with names from this period; that is especially true of south County Wexford which has it own typical names, like Sinnott, Stafford, Rossiter, Codd, Hoare, Lambert. And from the time of the Normans up to the present day there has been a trickle of English and Welsh settlers, so that in every part of Ireland you will find names like Lawless, Lynnott, Barrett, Howell, Bowen, Price, Evans, Pilkington, Motherway, Allardyce, Robinson, Jennings, Shortall, Somers, Downes, Kent, Bates, Jackson, Adams and so on through a very long list.

Then we have the Scots. First the valiant and sturdy fighting men – the 'Gallowglasses' – hired by Irish prince and Norman baron alike, Sheehys and MacCoys, MacDonnells and MacSweeneys, Mac Cabes and MacCorleys, some of them bringing names inherited from the Norsemen who settled along the western islands of Scotland. Then the trickle of Scottish settlers that gave us Patterson, Fraser, Graham, Kerr, Stewart, Scott and many others especially numerous in the part of Ireland just across the sea from Scotland.

When Louis the Fourteenth of France drove out the Huguenots – Protestant Frenchmen – a number of them settled in Ireland. They were not very numerous, but they soon made a name for themselves in the cloth trade, especially in Dublin and Portarlington, bringing such names as Guerin, Le Fanu, Du Cros, Champion, La Touche, Saurin, Dubourdieu, Lefroy, La Fere, Trench and Blanc. Another group of refugees, the Palatines, came as a result of the same King Louis' wars in Germany, and in contrast to the Huguenot townsmen these Germans were farmers and were settled on the land in County Limerick, where the names Modler, Sparling, Bovenizer, Ruttle, Tesky, Switzer, Shire, Doube and Schumacher are still well known.

Change of language often means change of name as well, or at least a different spelling or pronunciation. We can look back to ancestors of several races with several languages, Gaelic, Norse, Norman-French, Welsh, English, Lowland Scots, Hebridean, Huguenot-French and German. Palatine Schmidt became Smith, Huguenot Blanc became Blong. The same name is McDonald in Scotland and MacDonnell in Ireland. Scottish Ogilvy is the same as Irish O'Gilvea. Quite a lot of confusion arose from attempts to produce a 'translation' of names. In the year 1465 a law was passed that all people with Irish names living in the 'English Pale', that is Counties Dublin, Louth, Meath and part of County Kildare, should take English-sounding names instead, 'of one towne, as Sutton, Chester, Trym, Skryne, Corke, Kinsale, or colour, as white, blacke, browne, or art or science, as smith or carpenter, or office, as cooke, butler,' and fines were prescribed for anyone who would not obey. This law does not seem to have had much effect, but it did change the names of some Irish families. As time went on more changes and distortions occurred. When education was not general many people could not spell their names, and officials such as landlords' stewards or court clerks used a sort of phonetic spelling, such as 'M'Ea' for MacCoy, 'O'Culliggine' for Colgan, or by substitution, an English word which seemed to translate the name, like 'Woods' for Ó Coill (the descendant of Coll) or 'Silke' for Ó Síoda. On the other hand, many Normans, Welsh and English families had already adopted Gaelic forms; FitzElicot became MacElligot, FitzHugelin turned into MacQuillin, some of the Berminghams took MacFeorais, some of the Bourkes took MacWilliam, some of the Barretts changed to MacFadden, some of the Stauntons to MacAleevy and so on.

In recent times there has been a return to the Gaelic fashion of name, so much that very many people feel they must have two different names, their 'Irish' name and their 'English' name. And many families are not quite clear as to the exact form of name borne by their ancestors, say five hundred years ago, and have recourse to a book or a dictionary to find out what their 'Irish' name should be. If your name is 'Green', you have a choice of Mac Grianna, Ó Grianna, Mac Gréine, Ó hUaithne, Mac Glasain, Ó hUidhrín, while all the time your real descent may be from an honest bowman called Robin atte Grene who marched behind Strongbow or Milo de Cogan, or your name 'English', which you put into Irish

as 'Inglis' may have been a seventeenth century translation of Mac Gallóglaigh, descendant of a Gallowgla who
was really a MacDonnell from the Hebrides.

And so, in any district or parish, you can find a key to
much of our long and complex history. Our family trees
have many branches, and if we are wise we shall take
equal pride in all of them.

Our Christian Names

Many of the Red Indian tribes of North America had a
rather convenient custom in the giving of personal names.
Children were given temporary names. A boy might be
called 'Little Mouse' until he was admitted to the full
status of a man; then he got his adult name which was in
some way related to his stature, his prowess or his wisdom. A stout fighter might be called 'Roaring Bull' and
a clever schemer 'Wily Fox'. But our system offers no
such opportunity of escaping from the name which was
given to us without our knowlegde or consent. We must
make the best of what we have, and be glad that few of
us suffer the fate of that scion of the Muldoon clan whose
benighted parents christened him 'Marmaduke', thus
condemning the poor child to a life of misery until the
bright day dawned when a schoolmate was inspired to
bestow on him the nickname of 'Stinker', on which a better, happier life began for him.

Most of the peoples of the world follow a system like
ours. A name is given to the young child, and he, or she,
keeps the same name all through life. It is usually given
on some important occasion. We get ours at baptism, and
call it our 'Christian name', and distinguish it clearly from
our family name. But in ancient times it appears that people were known by one name only. In the Bible we have
personages without any second name, such as Adam, Eve,
Abraham, Sara, Ruth, Moses and so on. Some of these
are still in use and are among the oldest names which we
can trace. In ancient Ireland, too, it seems that even the very
important people were content with one name only, like

Queen Maeve, Cuchulain, Bricriu, Déirdre, Oisín, Oscar and so on. Some of these worthies changed their names, as for instance Cuchulain, who was called Setanta until he slew the great hound and served as guard of the house of Culan the smith until a new watchdog could be found. It was this spell of guard duty that gave him the name of Cuchulain – Culan's Hound. Many people got names in ways like this, and it is likely that in very ancient times all personal names were nicknames, that is names which had a definite meaning and association with the persons who received them, coming from some mark or characteristic of the individual, names like 'Fionn' and 'Donn' because the person had fair or brown hair, 'Breac' or 'Ballach' because he was freckled, 'Broc' or 'Dael' or 'Colm' because the person's disposition reminded one of a badger, a beetle or a dove. Later the custom arose of naming the child after some relative or friend, after the grandfather or the kind neighbour or the lord of the district, and descriptive names were given to people whom they did not fit at all. A little boy might be called 'Fionn' or 'Colm' after his grandfather, and grow up to be quite black haired or with the disposition of a lion rather than that of a dove, and a little girl might be called 'Fionuala' – 'Fair Shoulders' and have a sallow complexion, or 'Maeve', which originally meant 'frenzied' and be as mild as milk.

We might think that the number of such descriptive names is limited, but in ancient Ireland there were many hundreds of them. Some of them have continued in use down to our own day and others have been revived in recent years, but most of them have died out long ago, and many of them would sound very odd to us, such as 'Dálredochair' or 'Garbhraethach'. Many of them look rather complicated and far-fetched. Imagine having to explain to strangers the origin of a name like 'Dubhdabhoireann' (the black-haired person from two rough districts) or 'Cúganmáthair' (the hound who has no mother). Luckily for the people of those far off days most of them were simpler and more easy to understand. 'Cormac' meant 'son of the chariot', 'Diarmaid' meant 'without envy',

'Fionnbharr' meant 'fair head', 'Donnshléibhe' meant 'the brown man from the moorland', 'Bláthnait' meant 'little blossom' and so on. Some names of this kind were borne by only one or two people and then fell out of favour, but others became very popular indeed. We can see in the lists of the old Irish saints that there were more than a hundred men of the name 'Colmán' (little dove) venerated as saints, as well as twenty 'Colms'. There were thirteen women saints named 'Lassar' and eight named 'Brighid'. There were twenty-two saints 'Senan', eighteen saints 'Cuimín' as well as three women saints 'Cumman', fourteen saints 'Faelán', ten saints 'Brendan', twelve saints 'Ronan', and on the ladies' side three saints 'Eithne', three 'Darerca', three 'Daire'. Indeed this repetition of popular names may be seen right through the martyrologies and lists of saints. Oddly enough the custom of naming a child after a saint was not established in those days, nor for long after. In the lists of Irish saints there is, for instance, only one Saint Patrick. This may have come from a feeling of reverence, for many peoples at different times and places show their respect for some great person by forbidding the mention of his name.

Nowadays we usually give a saint's name to a child at baptism, if only as a second Christian name, but this custom was unusual in ancient Ireland. The old names continued in use with very little change. There are thousands of old Irish names recorded in the Annals, the Lives of the Saints, the Martyrologies and other ancient books, but hardly any of them were brought in by Christianity. There are a very few taken from the Bible. There was an abbess of Kildare called Martha and two Saints Noe (Noah). The great abbot of Iona who wrote the life of his master Colmcille and did so much to improve the status of women was Adamnán, that is 'Little Adam', and there was a bishop Joseph of Tallaght, three Saint Daniels, and a Saint Philip. A few Roman names, like Januarius, Martin and Hilary are to be found among the Irish saints, and a few British or Saxon names like Hilda, Beirchert and Marnoc. But all these are names of saints and they may have been names taken when entering religion. Whatever their origin they were very rare, and they were not passed on by being given to children.

Christianity did give one dignified name-custom. Instead of calling the child after a saint, they used the form 'Servant of the Saint', and so we have 'Maelíosa', 'Maelmhuire' and 'Maelbhrighde', 'Giollaphádraig' and 'Giollapheadair', where 'Mael' and 'Giolla' mean the servant or the devotee of the holy person.

The next big influence came from the Norsemen. As we know, they came first as pirates and plunderers, but as time went on many of them settled in Ireland, became peaceful farmers, seamen or traders and adopted Christianity. They soon became bound to their Irish neighbours by ties of marriage and friendship, and they have left us a number of Christian names which are still in use, such as Olaf, Magnus (Manus), Ranald, Lochlain and Roderick (Rory).

The coming of the Normans heralded the greatest change of all. Outside of West Ulster there are very few places in Ireland where their influence did not leave its mark. From Antrim to Kerry and from Mayo to Wexford they marched and fought and settled down. They became part of the Irish scene and the Irish way of life. At times they and their Irish neighbours fought savagely, but this hostility was not permanent. After all, the Irish often fought savagely among themselves, and they thought none the less of the Normans because they were fighting men. And they did more than fighting. Many an Irish girl gave her hand to a Norman and many a Norman lord was proud to marry his daughter to an Irish chief. Before long exasperated officials of the English king were complaining bitterly that a great number of the Normans in Ireland had become more Irish than the Irish themselves. This was true, indeed, but it is equally true that whole areas of Ireland adopted much of the Norman way of thought and of life. We can still see its influence at work, and nowhere more than in the names we bear. For nearly all our more popular Christian names, both of men and of women, have come from the Normans, and more than a few from the Saxon, Welsh and Flemish soldiers who served the Norman chieftains.

Take the women's names. The Normans have left us Anna, Agnes, Alice, Catherine, Cecily, Eleanor, Evelyn, Honora, Isabella, Joan, Margaret and many others. When we remember that several names commonly regarded as Irish are really Norman, that Una is a form of Agnes, that Síle (Shiela) is Cecily, Léan is Eleanor, Eileen is Evelyn, Nóra is Honora, Sibéal is Isabel and Siobhán is Joan we see how widespread the Norman fashion became. In the same way a great number of men's names came from the same source. The Normans gave us John, William, Walter, Roger, Gerald, Maurice, Raymond, Myles, Richard, Robert, Geoffrey, Oliver, Hugo (Hugh), Henry, David, Pierse (Peter), Philip, Edward, Michael.

The old Irish seldom named their children after saints, but the Normans were very devoted to this custom, and we owe the popularity of many saint-names as much to the Normans as to the direct influence of the Church. It is Normans, strange to say, who popularised the name which is taken as the typical Irishman's name, Patrick. In the old Norman records, such as the Ormond Papers, we find many Normans or their English or Welsh followers called Patrick, while at the same time there is hardly a single instance of the name being given to a native Irishman. In the same way the Normans gave us James, Simon, Stephen, Benedict, Nicholas, Matthew and many others.

During the Middle Ages, the Irish lords, both Norman and native had the practice of bringing in bodies of fighting men from the Western Islands and Highlands of Scotland, the famous Gallowglas. Many of these who had served their lords well and lived to tell the tale were rewarded with farms of land or posts as stewards and wardens, and so settled down in Ireland. A few names like Sorley, Alasdair (Alexander), Coll and Randal are inherited from them. During the Middle Ages the Church, too, played a part in the fashion of names, as it gradually insisted more and more on the names of well-known saints being given to the children at baptism. This custom has meant that any saint to whom there is popular devotion will surely give his or her name to many children. In ancient times the names Mary and Brighid were almost unknown in Ireland; the Church popularised them in the later Middle Ages, together with Clare, Monica, Teresa, Barbara, Angela, Ursula, Gertrude and others. From the same source came many men's names, like Bartholonew, Paul, Christopher, Vincent, Bernard, Francis, Dominic, Augustine, Alphonsus and many others.

When England had recovered from the Hundred Years War with France and her own bitter, bloody and costly civil war, the Wars of the Roses, greedy eyes were turned towards Ireland, and Henry the Eighth and his daughters Queen Mary and Queen Elizabeth undertook the thorough conquest of Ireland and the reduction of native Irish, Norman and old English alike to the power and might of English law. From that time onwards English power and influence spread mightily in Ireland, and in its turn has left its impression on our name system as well as on so many other aspects of our everyday life. Numbers of English people settled in various capacities in Ireland, some were farmers, others were professional men, officials or landlords, and, like the Norsemen and the Normans before them, became part of Ireland. They brought in some typical English names, such as George, Victor, Wilfred, Jasper, Valentine and Sidney, Matilda, Charlotte, Arabella, Sophia, Belinda and Pamela, names which from time to time were fashionable in England and were reflected in fashion here.

Many of the English immigrants used Christian names taken from the Bible, especially from the Old Testament, such as Rebecca, Sarah, Susanna, Judith, Ester, Elizabeth, Isaac, Abraham, Joshua, Moses, Jonathan, Samuel and Ebenezer. Some of these have, in their turn, gone out of fashion in more recent times, but many are still flourishing. A further complication of names was brought about by the efforts of legal officers, landlords and others in authority when they tried to reduce Irish names to some form which they, ignorant as they were of Gaelic, could pronounce and understand. Many of the typical old Irish names which had survived now took on another form, which was often quite different to the original. Donncha became 'Denis', Tadhg was turned into 'Timothy' or 'Thaddeus', Conal, Conchubhar and Conn all blossomed forth as 'Cornelius', Donal became 'Daniel', Ailbhe was turned into 'Albert', Beircheart was re-christened 'Benjamin', Cathal and Cearbhal and Cathaoir and Sorley all became 'Charles', and Giolla na Naomh disappeared under 'Nehemiah'. Nor did the ladies fare any better. Gobnait was changed to 'Debora' or 'Abigail'. Sadhbh became 'Sabina' or 'Sarah', Siobhán – the Irish form of the Norman Joan – became 'Judith', and another Norman-Irish name Síle (Shiela) was recast as 'Julia'. This process is being reversed in our own day, but it is not surprising to find the works of Irish novelists of the last century full of names like 'Flurry' and 'Terence' and 'Judy' and 'Abby', all of which hide good Irish names. Perhaps the greatest sufferer was the name of the great abbess of Kildare, Saint Brighid; we have 'Delia' and 'Belinda' and 'Dinah' and 'Bettina' and several others.

As the years go on we continue to add to our stock of names. Many new ones come from more recently canonised saints of the Church, or from popular devotions. Thus we have Aloysius, Vincent, Stanislaus, Teresa, Imelda, Carmel, Assunta and many others. We have reached out over the sea to many other countries in a search for new names, especially for girls' names, to France for Jacquetta and Jacqueline, Yvonne, Josephine, Valerie, Micheline and Antoinette, to Spain for Inez and Dolores, Isabel and Esmeralda, to Wales for Enid, Winifred and Gwendolin, to Scotland for Caitriona and Janet and even to the Shetland Islands for Brenda. In some of our towns, although (luckily) not to the same extent as in America and Britain, we get the 'Cinema names' such as Shirley, Carol and Myrna. Popular novels, and magazines too, have added to our list of names, with Rowena, Zoe, Elaine, Wanda, and have made old names popular again.

The Irish literary revival and the work of the Gaelic League of fifty or sixty years ago brought about a revival of many of the older names, saving many names which were falling out of use and rescuing others from the obscurity of the dim past. Here again girls gained more than boys, with Eithne, Déirdre, Emer, Aideen, Gráine, Lasariona, Fionula, Meave, Neasa, and the less common ones like Dervila, Tallula, Aifric and Attracta. At this time too, many of the names mistranslated in the eighteenth and nineteenth centuries were restored, and Siobhán, Shiela, Gobnait, Conal, Dermot, Fionán, Cathal and many others emerged from their smokescreen into the light of day. And many people who had genuine English names, inherited from their forebears, adopted Irish forms – many of them rather inappropriate.

This use of equivalents or translations is a source of a great deal of variety in names. A girl named Mary may be called Máire, Marie, Miriam, Marion, Mimi, Molly, Marietta, Manon, Polly or May. Margaret may appear as Maighreád, Maggie, Marguerite, Margot, Madge, Meg, Rita, Gretta, Marjorie, Peggy or Maisie. Patrick may turn up as Paddy, Patsy, Pat, Padden, Patey, Páidín or Patten, and John as Jack, Jock, Jackie, Johnnie, Jake, Hank or Jenkin, and in translation as Seán, Eoin, Jean, Ivan, Juan, Giovanni, Hans, Evan, Ian with all the pet-forms and diminutives in various languages, Gianni and Seainín and Vanya and Hannes and Juanicito – the possibilities are almost endless.

The poet who asked 'What's in a name?' posed a very interesting question. There is a very great deal of history in our names, and, indeed, a lot of geography too.

Games at Wakes

To our modern way of thinking the idea of playing games as part of the ceremonial of honouring the dead is rather shocking. The pomp and splendour for our great ones, the bands and the escorts, the gun-carriage and the flags draped in black, the volleys and the funeral oration, and the quieter ceremonies for our own dead relatives, these are solemn, mournful, and in our conventions dignified. Songs and dances, sports and games, jokes and storytelling all seem very much out of place and more suited to a happy occasion; they are, we think, appropriate to the wedding or the birthday party, but on no account to the grief and solemnity of death. And yet, in so thinking, are we not merely applying the standards of our own time and our own fashion and trying to make it a general rule for all times and all places, as we are so apt to do in so many directions? If some great and respected man or woman comes from abroad to visit us, we celebrate the occasion with gay and cheerful ceremonies, with music and song, with games and holidays. Is it, then, so very incongruous that people in other times and places should celebrate in a merry or joyful way the passage of a dear friend, as they believed and as we believe, from this world to a very much better one?

Prayers for the dead and ceremonies associated with death and burial are part of our Christian way of life; they are not exclusively Christian; there are other religions with customs and ceremonial intended to help the dead in the next life. But there are aspects of death and burial other than the religious. There is the hope and the determination that the memory of the dead man will be honoured because of what he was and what he did in this life, that his standing in the community will be reflected by the dimensions of his funeral. There is also the necessity of consoling the bereaved relatives, of distracting them from their grief in various conventional ways. Most of our death and burial customs are directed towards one or more of these objects; Prayer for the soul of the dead, honour to his memory and sympathy for his people. To our ancestors the playing of games at wakes offended against none of these.

What the origin of wake games may have been we shall never know. Was it merely a wish to while away the long hours of watching over the corpse? Was it a desire to amuse and distract the sorrowing family of the dead man? Or was it some survival from remote time, some ancient pagan ceremonial which had already become a mere harmless convention by the time that Christianity first came to Ireland? We do not know; we may speculate as we wish, and devise all sorts of interesting theories without getting any nearer to the answer to the question: what began it all? But we do know that a century ago it was the usual practice in many parts of Ireland that games were played at wakes, and that traces of the custom survived until quite recently, so that people still alive remember the playing of these games. We also know that these games were not regarded in any way inappropriate to the occasion or disrespectful to the dead. Quite the opposite; they were a necessary part of the wake – to omit them would be an offence to the dead person's memory, and if there was no indication that they were going to be performed, the chief mourner or some other person close to the dead man would ask a neighbour to begin them.

In the old days the corpse was waked usually for two nights, sometimes for three. Nowadays the coffin is taken to the church the night before the burial, and it may be that there is no wake at all, for if a person dies before daybreak, the body is carried to the church the same evening, and remains in the house overnight only in the case of those who die during the day. A convention of my native district refers to the house of the dead person as the 'corpse-house' during the day and the 'wake-house' during the night. No amount of visiting by sympathising friends and neighbours during the day constitutes a wake; only the watching over the corpse during the hours of darkness is a wake. Furthermore, it is the custom that women, very old people and children visit the house only during the day, so that those present at the wake, that is the night watch over the corpse, are almost all men. This was even more the case in former times, and so it came about that the wake games, played only during the wake proper, were performed by men. In our locality certain of the neighbours were asked to help at the wake, one distributed pipes and tobacco, another doled out whiskey, a third took charge of the porter keg, and a fourth was charged with regulating the wake games. The mood of the wake varied very much from one case to another. Where the circumstances were tragic, the death of the breadwinner or of the young mother, there was real grief and the wake games, if played, were half hearted. But in the case of an old person, whose death was in the ordinary nature of things, the grief was more restrained and the old customs were observed with enthusiasm. Indeed, some such wakes were no more than social entertainments. Witness the case of the man, in our parish, who was entering the wake-house when some *dailtín* threw a *ciarán* of turf at him; he turned and said: 'Be it known to you that I came here to enjoy myself as well as the next man, and not for any blackguarding!' It was at wakes like this that the wake games flourished. Our district, however, was one of those in which wake games had died out; the old people had heard of them in former times, but very few of them had seen them; their place had been taken by card games, parlour tricks, fortune telling, stories and the making and reciting of verses. But they did survive in other places until quite recently.

Some of them were tests of strength or skill, such as holding a brush handle knee high in both hands and jumping over it. A favourite test was to seat a boy on a wooden chair, then stick a pin in the back of one of the back legs, about two inches above the floor, and then tell the boy seated on the chair to pull the pin with his teeth without putting either foot on the floor; his contortions in trying to do this were highly entertaining. The 'cobbler's dance' in which the performer squatted down on his 'hunkers' and danced like a Cossack was another favourite test of skill. 'Hands down' was a test of strength in which two men sat facing each other across a narrow table, each resting an elbow on the table, their hands clasped palm to palm; the test was to push the other man's down until his knuckles touched the table. In another form of this, the contestants' little fingers were hooked together and each strove to pull the other's hand down. In another contest two sweeping brushes were obtained, two men sat on the floor with their hands clasped about their knees and a brush was pushed in under each man's knees above his forearms, and then they fought by trying to bang each other with the head of the brush. The 'sudden lift' was performed by four men lifting a fifth. One man, to be lifted, was seated on a chair. The other four gathered round, the first slapped his open palm on the table, the second slapped his palm on the back of the first man's hand, to be followed by the third and fourth, and as soon as the fourth hand slapped down all four turned, thrust their right forefingers two under the elbows and two under the knees of the seated man, and lifted him into the air. To one who had not seen it before, this was an astonishing feat. Sometimes the man to be lifted was not seated but lying flat on the floor. There were many feats and tests of this kind.

But, to come to the formal games: some of them were ordinary children's games, such as were played, and still are, in any school yard, games like 'tig' and 'four corner-ed fool', or indoor games like 'Jack is alive' or 'púicín'. One of the most widely played was 'shuffle the bróg' or 'hunt the slipper'. The players were seated on the ground in a circle, and in the middle sat one who had been count-ed out or otherwise chosen; the seated ones passed the 'bróg' or 'slipper' around behind their backs while the one in the middle had to guess where it was. While the 'bróg' (which might be any small object) was passing, all the members of the circle pretended to be passing it, with such exclamations as *'thart an bróg!'* 'around with it!' 'give it here to me!' 'I have it!' and so on, to confuse the guesser, who, if he failed to guess it in a certain time, might be subjected to some forfiet or penalty. Many wake games, much more so than children's games or the child-ren's way of playing, were designed to involve one or other of the players in embarrassing or humiliating situa-tions; if he bore these with good humour, he gained in the general esteem, if he could turn the joke against his persecutors he was generally applauded, but if he lost his temper he went down in everybody's estimation. Thus, in the game of the 'bee-hive' or 'gathering the honey', the poor 'gom' selected as the 'hive' was drenched by mouthfuls of water collected by the 'bees'. In 'shoeing the horse' the victim had to hold up his foot while the 'smith' hammered the sole of his shoe severely – this might be done to some young fellow who was showing off a new pair of shoes. In another game each participant was questioned by the master; he could answer what he liked, but he must not say 'yes', 'aye' or 'no'; the master tried in all ways to make him say one of these words, and if he did, he was severely thumped or otherwise punished. 'The tailor' was another game in which somebody was 'caught out'; the 'tailor' announced that he must measure those present for new clothes, and each had to stand up, squat down, bend, raise his arms or legs while the 'tailor' took all sorts of comical measurements. The climax of the game came when a selected victim, told to stretch up his arms, had a can of water poured down his sleeve by a boy hidden in the loft overhead. In 'hurly-burly', each player had to guess how many fingers the leader held up, and was severely thumped until he guessed the correct number. A similar game was 'goat's horns up' in which the leader recited a rhyme ending in these words, changing the name of the animal each time; when he named a horned animal the others had to hold up their forefingers, and when they failed to do this or held the fingers up when an animal without horns was named, they were thumped or otherwise punished.

There were other games which were only seen at wakes, some of which seem to have been of a very peculiar nature, so much that they were condemned and forbidden by the clergy, some of them specifically by name, for instance one called 'Fronsy fronsy' by the bishop of Leighlin in 1748. Indeed, there is a long series of condemnations by the Church, reaching back over at least three hundred years, of all disrespectful and unchristian practices at wakes, such as songs, music, games and uncouth behaviour of any kind. The wonder is that these customs persisted so long: they must have been very deeply founded in tradition to have survived as they did.

The Blacksmith

There is a passage in the Ancient Laws of Ireland referring to the question of straying or trespassing cattle and horses; these must be impounded and notice must be given at the more important places of popular resort, namely, the house of the local lord, the house of the judge, the local church and the forge. This shows that the forge was in ancient times, as it was up to quite recently, a place where people gathered and where news could easily be spread. In those days, a thousand years or so ago, the forge was situated, as it still is, beside a road, preferably near or at a crossroads, and close to running water, and the passers-by were just as eager to drop in for a chat, so that the forge was never without its group of men and boys, some of them waiting their turn with a piece of work for the smith, others just idling away the time. The fact that women seldom came near the forge, and that, if they did come with some job for the smith, they hardly ever entered and usually went away quickly, made it something of a men's club. And up to quite recently, as in ancient times when he was the social equal of the judge and the poet, the smith was the most important of the rural craftsmen, and a leading man in his community.

We are told that a tailor who boasted that his craft was the oldest in the world, claiming that the first tailor was the one who sewed clothes of figleaves for Adam and Eve, was put to shame by a smith who wanted to know who made the needle that sewed the leaves? For the smith boasted that he made all the tools of all the trades, and the tools of his own trade as well. Certainly the smith of a few generations ago, of the days before the industrial revolution had flooded the world with factory-made articles, made a very large number of items. For the farmer he made spades, plough-irons, shovels, sleans, forks, axes, mattocks, scythes, billhooks, gates, and many other implements; for the housewife not only pots, griddles, candlesticks, and fire-irons, but knives and forks, scissors, shears, needles and pins, as well as locks, bolts and hasps, hinges, screws, nails and window bars to furnish the house. He made the tools of twenty different trades as well as iron fittings for the mason, the carpenter, the wheelwright and the boat builder. A master smith of a century ago could make at least a hundred different items; his greatgrandfather of a century earlier made twice that number, including in his repertoire a whole series of weapons for hunting and warfare.

The good smith, we are told, had an eye sharper than the tailor's measure. He could, for instance, tell at a glance and to within an inch the length of iron required for the band of a wheel. He was a patient craftsman; such tasks as the assembling of an iron gate might take a couple of hours of unbroken work, and seldom did that length of time pass without the arrival of some customer with an exaggerated sense of the urgency of his own needs. Almost invariably he was regarded as a rock of commonsense, one whose advice on all sorts of questions was sought and valued, yet often among the men gathered at the forge was some opinionated fellow who did not hesitate to contradict the smith even in matters appertaining to his own trade. And there was, and still is, the kind of person who brings to be repaired some shoddy article which the smith himself could have made so much better in the first place. A patient, kindly, respectable man was the smith, and a man, too, with deep roots in the community, for his craft was hereditary with son following father in the same locality, usually in the same forge; many a smith could trace his ancestry back for five or six generations of ironworking ancestors. Even in his Sunday clothes you could tell a smith on sight; he was likely to be a powerfully built man of great strength, cleanshaven even when beards were in fashion and with the pale complexion of the man who did much work in poor light, this latter by choice, for the knowledge of the various properties of glowing iron was part of his skill and a degree of darkness was necessary to observe this. In the long winter evenings, when he worked on the making of implements, cranes for the farmhouse kitchens, gates and others of his products which took time in the fashioning, he worked by the glow of his fire or, at most, by the light of a bogdeal splinter. And on such cold evenings the warmth of the forge drew a group of the local men who sat about discussing the news of the day and the political situation, deferring to the smith's opinion and ready to give a hand to assist him and his work-men.

His powerful hands, which could swing a sledgehammer mightily or lift the anvil from its block with the left while he held the hammer in his right – one of his typical feats of strength – were also very skilful. He could repair a clock or make a fish hook, sew a broken china dish or shape a top-spear for a small boy as readily as he could make a scythe blade or a smoothing iron. We are told that the apprentice smith was expected to make the *seachrán sriana*, a sort of wire puzzle which required great skill in forging, before he was considered a trained craftsman. His hands were very gentle, too, for he was a healer whose gifts were at the service of ailing man and beast. Above all he was expert in the care of horses. He could tell the exact height of any horse or pony by looking at it, or its age by a glance at its teeth. He could tell if a horse was badly fed or weaned too soon or overworked. He treated glanders, farcey and strangles, ready to lance and cauterise swellings or to flush out the horse's nose or mouth with a syringe which he made from a pig's bladder and a short length of hollow elder twig. He treated saddle and harness sores and spavins with plasters and washes of which a major ingredient was the water from the stone trough in which he cooled and tempered his hot irons. He pulled horses' teeth with specially made forceps and compounded draughts to cure broken wind, and none could give a horse-ball as well as he. When necessary he bled horses, using an instrument called a fleam, like a pocket knife with a small triangular projection on the blade, which was tapped with a little stick to pierce the vein and draw the blood.

The smith was the dentist of the locality, his usual method of tooth extraction being the tying of the offending tooth by a strong string to the anvil and the sudden presensation of a red hot iron to the victim who then pulled his own tooth. But an old man of my acquaintance told me that he saw a man being held by two others while the smith pulled a tooth with a specially shaped iron forceps; it was said also that the smith would place a small block of wood against the tooth and tap with a hammer to loosen it up. Some smiths pulled teeth with their fingers; some are alleged to have used the horse-shoe tongs, and it is probably one of these who whipped out a patient's tooth only to be told that it was the wrong one. '*Is cuma dhuit, a dhuine, nách ag réiteach chuige a bhíos* – never mind, man, I was clearing the way to it' said the unperturbed craftsman.

He treated other ailments, too, especially skin troubles, warts, boils and eruptions, for which the forge water applied by the smith was a wellknown cure. People came to the forge for bottles of the water for use by those who themselves could not come. Men with cut or sprained hands would drop in when passing by, and dip the injured hand in the trough. It was very good for styes in the eye, and would, it was said, even cure a squint provided that it was applied unseen by the smith on three mornings in succession.

By longstanding tradition in some localities the smith had a standing arrangement by which he gave regular service in shoeing horses and repairing equipment for the farmers in return for regular deliveries to him at set intervals of produce such as oats, potatoes, flour, vegetables and so on. This may have been a relic of the ancient days when the community supported the master craftsman so that the latter could spend all his time on his craft. Another ancient tradition which continued down into our own century was the giving to the smith of the head of any beast killed for meat by the farmer. In our district this custom had a little twist to it; the farmer gave the smith the head of the killed pig, but the smith had made pig-rings for all the farmer's pigs in return. If the smith was very busy, as he usually was in spring and harvest, the local men formed a *meitheal*, a working party, to sow, plant and reap for him, so that he did not have to leave the work of the forge; 'as big as a smith's *meitheal*' was said of a large gathering of people. Other services, such as a horse and cart to draw his turf, a load of manure or free grazing for his cow were given to the smith in return for his regular care for horses and implements. New implements were usually paid for in money, and in some places the customer was expected to bring his own iron. But money seldom changed hands at the forge in the old days; the fair day was when the smith was paid – he went early to the fair and the farmers settled up with him when their cattle were sold. Generally the smith was a sober man, but his return from town late on the fair-day evening was usually musical and merry, as people for whom he had done little jobs often stood him a drink or too in lieu of cash payment. Being himself always gener-ous with his help in case of need, he hated nothing more that a mean customer. There is the tale of how the smith outwitted the mean farmer by telling him that all he would pay for the set of horse-shoes was a farthing for the first nail, a halfpenny for the second, a penny for the third, and so on, to which the farmer agreed, thinking it a bar-gain. Imagine his horror when he found that the bill was over £50,000!

No wonder that it was sometimes whispered that the smith, who was master of such varied skill and knowledge, was in touch with powers outside of nature. It was well known that he could lay charms and spells, though al-ways for a good purpose, such as the cure of illness. He worked all day with iron, and it was common knowledge that iron was a safeguard against the powers of evil. He could set at nought the evil spells laid to steal the pro-duce from the fields or the butter from the dairy; this he accomplished by a liberal sprinkling of the forge wa-ter, accompanied by the appropriate words which were known only to himself. He could cut and sear a sore on a horse's back or leg, and the horse stood quietly for him all through the operation. No ordinary man could do things like this. And wasn't it well known that the smith's curse on the oppressor or the evildoer, especially if solemnly pronounced by three or, better still, by seven smiths while one of their number turned the anvil, was more than enough to avenge any wrong.

We are told that Saint Patrick prayed against the spells of smiths, but that was in the days when christianity was wrestling with paganism. Of later smiths in tale and tra-dition there is very little which is not good, and even then the fall from grace is not by the master smith but by some rude or careless apprentice, like the one in the tale of Saint Lasariona. As a young girl she was being trained in a convent, and the mother abbess sent her each morning to the local smithy for a coal to light the convent kitchen fire, and so innocent was she that when the kindly master smith laid the burning coal on her outstretched apron the cloth was not burned. Until one morning when the old smith was away and his apprentice, in giving her the coal remarked 'Miss, you have very nice ankles' and when she gave way to a feeling of pride at this praise the apron straightaway caught fire. There is a certain townland in County Cork, the scene of this happening, and we are told that never since that day can a smith, no matter how skilled, weld iron within its boundaries.

The Fair Day

'And take care' says Jack's mother to him, and he setting out for the fair in the dark of the morning 'would you take anything less than the highest penny in the fair for the red yearling!' But, as the tale goes on to tell us, poor Jack was not to be numbered among the intellectual giants of that fabulous age, and when he came to the fair green and announced that he must have the highest penny, didn't a rogue of a dealer hold a penny up in the air on the point of his ashplant, and poor simple Jack parted with the heifer. Many a folktale begins in this way; the poor widow has only the one little animal to sell, and her son sets out for the fair, full of hope of a good bargain, and that is the beginning for him of marvellous adventures. And no wonder, for the day of the fair was a most important occasion in the country peoples' round of work and play. Everyone, says the proverb, should go to the fair, whether he had business there or not.

Our ancient records give us a glimpse of the great fairs of a thousand or fifteen hundred years ago. Such assemblies were held periodically at Tara, Tailtean, Uisneach,

Carman and other places, and large throngs of people came together there. The kings and nobles held high council, treating of peace and war, tribute, hostages and alliances. Everybody with anything to sell or to buy was sure to be there, and bargaining went on from morning until night. Most of the people, however, were in search of entertainment, and entertainment of all kinds was there for the poor as well as for the rich. An old account of the fair of Carman (now Wexford) tells us that forty seven kings and high nobles attended with all their followers and retainers, as well as a great concourse of ordinary people. The fair lasted for six days, and each day there were races, sports and contests of various kinds; one afternoon was set aside for contests between the ladies, and the Men of Leix had the special task of seeing to the arrangements for these, and for guarding the ladies' cloaks and jewellery while they took part in the games. Musicians, poets and storytellers were there, and bands of jugglers, tricksters and clowns. Special parts of the field were set apart for a cattle and horse fair, for the sale of food and clothing, and for the booths of the foreign merchants who displayed luxury goods such as jewels, silk, wine, pepper and other products of the 'Eastern World'. Armed guards patrolled the ground, making sure that there was no disorder, and any breach of the peace was severely punished. Each evening these guards signalled the end of the day's activities by clashing their spears together, and on that signal all trading and entertainment had to stop, and the multitude dispersed. Most of them, no doubt, camped in the open, under tents or little wattle and sod huts at the rapid making of which the people of the time were expert. Some may have slept under their carts or chariots, and, anyhow, this fair was held at Lúnasa, the beginning of August, and so the weather cannot have been very cold. There were special places for parking the vehicles, and rules about careful driving; we are told in the *Annals of the Four Masters*, that at the last fair of Tailteann, in the year 1168 on the eve of the Norman invasion, the line of horses and vehicles reached a distance of six miles, and with such crowded roads some regulation of traffic was necessary. The fair of Carman, and other fairs too, began in Christian times with public Mass and other religious celebrations; these may have taken the place of ancient pagan rites associated with the fair.

The coming of the Normans increased if anything the number and importance of the fairs. The king of England, who claimed the Lordship of Ireland and controlled some of that country, had the pleasant habit of granting the tolls of fairs to various officers or courtiers, sometimes even to a church or abbey, and the early Norman documents give some information, in connection with these grants, about fairs. Permission to hold an eight-day fair at Dublin at the beginning of May was granted in 1204, no doubt an ancient fair of Bealtaine. In the same document the eight-day fairs at Waterford from the First of August (Lúnasa), and at Limerick from Martinmas (11 Nov.) are mentioned. An eight-day fair at Swords, County Dublin, beginning on the eve of the feast of Saint Colmkille, patron of the town, is mentioned in 1213, as are a great fair at Clonmel on the feast of All Hallows in 1225 and one in Ferns on May Eve in 1226. The association of the fair with the festival day is clearly shown. The great ancient fairs were held at Bealtaine or Lúnasa or Samhain. Tailtean and Carman were at Lúnasa (1 August); many of the medieval towns had fairs on that day, and in our own day the most famous Irish fair, the Puck Fair at Killorglin is at Lúnasa (old style) moved up eleven days in the month by a peculiar provision of the Act which accepted the Gregorian calendar in Britain and Ireland in 1750, which ordered that the fairs should be held on the 'natural day' and not on the festival day as in the old calendar observance. This seems to have been a deliberate attempt to separate the fair from the festival and it certainly reduced the importance of such gatherings as that at Kilmihil, County Clare, on Michaelmas or at Nantenan, County Limerick, on Saint James's Day, by prohibiting buying and selling on these days and ordering the fair to be held eleven days later.

This was by no means the first attempt of officialdom

at changing the old customs associated with the fairs. In the year 1431 the Parliament of Ireland noted with some misgiving that divers Irish enemies of their Lord the King did raise and hold amongst themselves certain fairs and markets, and that it was the painful fact that certain of his majesty's subjects, and even English lieges, did resort thereto, and sell and buy divers merchandises, whereout the said enemies did take profits, customs and benefits, to the great injury of the burghs and market towns. It was the old Irish custom to hold fairs at places out in the countryside, a custom which, indeed, has come down to recent times at, for instance, Old Kilcullen, Ballyagran in County Limerick, and the great horse fair at Cahirmee. The townsmen did not like these fairs, which brought them no toll or custom, and did their best to get the officials to discourage or forbid them, and in many cases succeeded. Some of the country fairs survived, however, probably because they were too important to suppress, and the townsmen had to come to terms with them. We find Roger Lacy, sheriff of Limerick, in the year 1295, promising to pay a debt of 20 shillings at the Fair of Aney, that is, of Knockainy, County Limerick, which was one of the ancient assemblies. That the sherrif and his merry men paid some attention to the regulation of the fairs and the protection of the people at them is shown by the hue and cry raised at the fair of Tallaght in the same year, 1295, after those who slew a certain poor man, Simon Ó Cormaic, on his way to the fair, and plundered him of two draught oxen and five shillings in silver; the slayer was brought to justice, but pleaded that Simon had himself stolen the cattle and that he killed him to recover them.

That the progress of merchants to a fair was not always free of peril is shown by the case of the servant man of one Will Douce, a merchant of Dublin. This servant was in charge of a pack-horse laden with goods on the way to the fair of Kilkenny in the year 1304, but, in the town of Naas, he fell in with a lady who rejoiced in the name of Christine la Sadelhackere; what transpired is not quite clear, but in the morning a box containing linen cloth, shoes and hose, value twenty pence, was missing from the horse's pack, and the whole affair was thrashed out in open court, much to the annoyance of all parties concerned.

It is quite probable that in very few years' time the old style of fair will have been quite superseded by the cattle mart; this has happened already in many centres. If the fairs die out, a lot of old custom and tradition will die with them, because such important occasions drew about them all sorts of usages and beliefs, some of them commonsense and practical, some very strange. All the conventions of striking the bargain had to be followed; by doing so the buyer could attribute all sorts of faults to the beast he wanted to buy, while the seller could remark freely on the buyer's meanness, all without offence to either. There always was a third party standing by to help the bargain along. 'Ah, now, have sense for yourself, that is a good beast, and you have sense too, 'tisn't a bad price the man is offering you. Come on, now, don't break my word! split the difference' and so on. Often the buyer would walk away, fully expecting to be called back; often the seller would loudly proclaim that he wasn't selling at the price offered, but usually the margin of difference was narrowed until the bargain was made. Then the buyer spat on the palm of his hand and slapped it on the seller's palm, the money was paid over and the cow marked with the buyer's mark. A larger transaction meant a walk to the bank where the financial end was settled, and this called also for at least one quick one in the nearby pub, where the third party who had helped to make the bargain was not forgotten.

In most parts of the country a 'luck-penny' was given with the sold beast, a small sum, a couple of shillings or so, in proportion to the price, by the seller to the buyer, and in our district this money had to come from the sale of eggs; when the husband or son was setting out for the fair, the housewife always had a few shillings of the egg-money ready to give him for the luck-penny. It was lucky for the man bringing beasts to a fair to have some bit of iron or steel, especially a steel knife, in his pocket.

It was lucky to shake a grain of salt or a pinch of ashes on the animals to be sold, as well as holy water. And it was very unlucky to meet a hare or a red haired woman first thing on the road. And when the beast was sold, if it had a headstall, a rope or a spancel from the house, this had to be taken off and brought home, for fear that the luck of the house might go with it. Some people threw an old shoe after those going to a fair, to bring them good fortune.

'Even if all you have is an old puck goat, be in the middle of the fair with him' is an old saying. The 'middle of the fair' was where the main part of the buying and selling was done, but it was around the edge that the crowds gathered as the day went on. Most of the important buying and selling of livestock was over by the middle of the morning; the farmers, drovers and buyers had been there since the dawn, and most of the cattle were sold and moving off. But now the farmers' wives, the children and the servant boys and girls were coming in for the day's fun. There were pedlars and cheap-jacks with 'standings' full of clothes and boots, small house furnishings and trinkets to tempt money out of purses. There were other standings, as well as the shops, with gooseberries, apples and plums, crubeens and meat pies, 'say-grass' and periwinkles, sweets and sugar-stick and gingerbread. There were tents where you could get a cup of tea or a drink, and other tents for dancing. There were pipers, fiddlers and fluteplayers, and ballad singers bawling their songs and selling rudely printed 'ballets' at a penny a time. At the bigger fairs there were swing-boats and merry-go-rounds and cock-shots or 'maggies' as they were called – crude wooden effigies at which you got 'three shots a pinny and five for tuppence', with a prize if you knocked one of them down. Sometimes the cock-shots were bottles, sometimes clay pipes to be broken by a lucky throw, and sometimes a man who popped his head up out of a barrel and shouted insults at the throwers. There were tinkers, tramps and beggars, the trick-of-the-loop man and the three-card man and the thimblerigger. All the children had been saving pennies for the big day, and the relatives whom they met were sure to give them a 'fairing' – a small present. The servant boys and girls had the day off 'only to be home in time to milk the cows', and a proportion of their wages to spend.

Some fairs were famous for the hiring of servants and labourers, and the *spailpíní* from the west gathered at certain known spots were the farmers came and bargained with them for the spring or harvest work. Other fairs were known places for the making of matches and marriage settlements. Faction fights were a regular feature of some fairs; it was unwritten law that the factions kept quiet until well on in the day, but there were places which considered themselves disgraced if evening came without a blow struck. And in the bad old days the rulers of the land considered the fair the ideal place to over-awe the assembled people by shows of armed force, reading of proclamations and, often, the flogging or hanging of some poor fellow who had fallen foul of the law. It was on a fair day in the year 1766 that Father Nicholas Sheehy was hanged, drawn and quartered at Clonmel, and his head set on a spike over the jail gate.

The Oldest Friend

One day towards the end of the last century the bellman of Newcastlewest went through the town on a fair day announcing that large numbers of donkeys were required by the British Government for some expedition into a desert area of Africa. Most of the listeners thought the idea very funny and that the whole thing was a joke, and on the appointed day only a few simple countrymen arrived with donkeys for sale. But sure enough the buyers were there and the scarcity of donkeys brought good prices to the great disappointment of those who regarded the matter as a hoax. About a year later the bellman was heard again announcing this time that Vast Numbers of Dogs were Needed for Clearing Rats out of West Africa and naming the day when the official buyers would attend.

And on the appointed day a large throng from town and country assembled in the square and the market field in Newcastlewest with hundreds of dogs of all sizes and breeds, but as the day wore on and no buyers appeared it slowly dawned on the dog-sellers that this was really a hoax. Most of them were so disgusted that they abandoned their dogs in the town, and though some of the dogs found their way back home very many of them joined in packs and terrorised the town and the countryside around in their frantic hunt for something to eat. One old resident who owned a shop in the Market Street used to tell of how a pack invaded the shop and devoured fourteen pigs' heads and a 56-pound firkin of butter before he could summon enough help to eject them.

For months the packs were on the prowl. The R.I.C. turned out with their carbines and shot many of them, and any farmer who owned a shotgun was asked to join in the hunt. One of my grand-uncles killed three of them one night with an ancient muzzle loader well charged with buckshot when a pack of about twenty of them invaded his farmyard. Dogs were unpopular in the district for quite a while afterwards, for more than one honest working dog ran away and joined forces with the outlaws.

Such events are, happily, rare. Indeed this appears to be the only large dog-market ever held in Ireland, and runaway dogs were very seldom in such numbers that they became a menace to life and property on a large scale. Not that the old days were without their own excitement, for wolves were still to be found in Ireland up to, say, two hundred years ago, and although most of the evidence indicates that they were slinking thieves on the lookout for an unguarded calf or sheep, they sometimes appeared in packs and became a real danger. It was against these pests that the dog proved his worth and gained fame and honour; there is passing mention of herding dogs and of ladies' lap-dogs in the old literature, but pride of place is given to the wolfhounds, from the great hound slain by Cúchulainn down to the champions of our own day. The names of the hounds of Finn and Oisín ring through the ballads of the Fianna, and Oisín worried Saint

Patrick with questions as to whether his favourite hound would be waiting for him in Heaven. Patrick himself had escaped from slavery in Ireland in a ship carrying wolfhounds to Europe, and only a few years earlier the Roman Consul Quintus Aurelius wrote a letter to his brother Flavianus thanking him for sending seven great Irish hounds and telling of the astonishment of the Roman crowd at their size and fierce aspect. Their fame spread all over Europe and even farther. A Scandinavian chronicler tells of a raiding expedition into Ireland in which the Vikings rounded up a great herd of cattle. Then came a poor farmer to beg the Viking chief to give him back his few poor cows, only to be told that he could have them if he could pick them out from the hundreds of beasts in the herd. Not a bit perturbed the farmer whistled up his hound, and the big dog ran in and cut them out of the herd so quickly that the raiders were amazed. Many wolfhounds found their way to Norway and Denmark as valuable prizes in the Viking ships. They were great favourites in England. The Spanish poet Lope de Vega wrote a sonnet in praise of one of them, and requests came from the Kings of Spain, Sweden and Poland, the Sultan of Turkey, the Shah of Persia and the Great Mogul, asking for Irish wolfhounds.

It is more than likely that the first men who penetrated into Ireland brought dogs with them, and ever since they have been the best friends and helpers of the farmer, the huntsman and the householder, set apart from other animals by their courage, their fidelity and their sagacity. In recent times the sheepdogs are the most useful and the most prized. Once, at the Fair of Puck I saw a farmer from the Glencar side refusing an offer of £100 for his collie; although he was a poor man he would not think of parting with the dog, but he consoled the would-be buyer with the promise of a trained pup. I knew of another collie in West Kerry who used to bring his master's animals unaided to Dingle fair; the master, a mountain farmer, put the cattle on the road in charge of the dog and followed on to the fair a couple of hours later, sure that he would find the beasts outside a certain house on the street of Dingle. As soon as the animals were sold he rewarded the dog with a pound of minced beef and then told him to be off home, again quite sure that the dog would be there in the farmyard on his return. No wonder that dogs like these were highly regarded.

During the past thirty years or so greyhounds have become more popular and numerous than ever before because of the spread of greyhound racing. Coursing has been a favourite sport for centuries, and great dogs like Master Magrath were famed far and wide. But in many parts of the country the landlords would not allow their tenants to keep greyhounds, as they insisted that all hunting rights belonged to themselves; thus greyhounds were rare in many districts until recently. The greyhound has exceptional speed, but is not renowned either for intelligence or courage, and poachers and huntsmen used to cross the greyhound with sturdier breeds in the hope of getting a dog with bravery and wit as well as speed. Another type of cross breed valued by many was the 'half-fox', a hybrid between a male fox and a terrier bitch; these were said to be wild, unruly and vicious, but full of courage and fight, ready to go down a hole and challenge a fox or a badger.

The old people used to say that the proper way to test the courage of young pups was to offer them a fox's skin. If a pup ignored it, he would never make a hunting or a fighting dog, but if he bristled up and snapped at it, he had the right drop in him. For hunting hares the best hound of all, they said, was a black one without a single white hair, but the greyhound was not much good for the fox as he was not brave enough, and the fox knew this and would show fight to the greyhound when he would do so to no other dog. The big brown terrier and the Kerry Blue were the dogs with the intelligence to outwit the fox and the strength and courage to fight and kill it. Small terriers, like the Glen Imail, would not hesitate to attack a fox or a badger, but lacked the fighting weight and might be killed or maimed by the bigger animal, so the huntsmen made sure to have good big dogs with the good little ones. In parts of south

Kerry and south west Cork you may still find a beagle on nearly every farm, for draghunts and beagling are still popular in that area, with the devotees following the pack on foot for miles over the roughest country. Sometimes on a moonlight night you can hear these big dogs baying at the moon, a musical but very melancholy sound, enough to frighten the wits out of a nervous person hearing it for the first time. A city man once told me that he ran nearly a mile with the fright one night when he was walking alone and heard the Scarteen Black and Tans baying the moon.

The old people claimed that a dog could see ghosts and spirits invisible to humans. If a dog backs away growling from something which we cannot see, well, there you are! Doesn't that prove it? And many the tale was told about some dog warning his master of the unseen menace so that he escaped in time, although some of the stories went on to tell of how the brave dog was found dead next morning. Dogs can sense death approaching, we were told, and if you hear a dog howling in the night without cause, you may expect the worst. One family, the O'Keeffes of West Cork, had a phantom hound of its own, the 'Gaidhirín Caoimh', and this creature's plaintive howl caused every dog in the district to join in, so that the whole countryside was ringing with the mournful sound to tell of the coming death of an O'Keeffe of the old stock. Other ghostly hounds there are which haunt certain places, and these are avoided or quickly passed at night. These apparitions, we were told, do not try to harm the passers by, but their aspect is horribly frightening and their appearance is a certain omen of some bad fortune to come.

You should always talk to a dog in a friendly way, but you should never ask him a question directly, for what would you do if he answered you, as well he might? And, although you should say 'God bless it' of every living thing, you should never say it of the dog. A tale was told to explain why this should be so. There was a priest long ago in a certain parish in County Kerry who was a great lover of singing and music. Not a piper or a fiddler or a ballad singer passed that way without being entertained right well at the presbytery, and the priest used to call the neighbours to listen to the music and song. One night, whatever, the priest was summoned to the bedside of a dying man in a lonely glen, and he set out on foot as the path was too rough for a horse. And suddenly, as he was passing a big clump of sallies, he heard a voice raised in song, the sweetest voice he ever had heard, singing 'Cailín Deas Crúite na mBó'. He stopped to listen, and so sweet was the song that he lost track of time and place and only could think of how he might find the sweet singer. He left the path and went into the sallies and there, God bless the mark! was a huge black dog with red eyes glaring, sitting on its haunches with its head up, singing. Stricken with horror the priest remembered the dying man and hurried along as fast as he could. But the man was dead when he reached the house, and when he reckoned the time he found that he must have been a full three hours listening to that unhallowed minstrel. Thereupon he decreed that never again should any Christian say 'God bless it' of a dog.

The dog's tongue was believed to hold a certain cure for cuts and sores. Didn't the dog lick his own wounds, and didn't they always heal cleanly? So if you had a cut or a sore that would not heal, you should let the dog lick it as often as possible, and it would heal quickly. On the other hand, the bite of a dog would never heal until the dog was killed; this belief often led to trouble when a valued dog was accused of biting somebody, and the owner refused to kill it. A 'wicked' dog, one which attacked people or chased cars or animals, was often restrained by having a block of wood or a stick hung from his neck; this was not heavy enough to do him any harm but it banged against his front legs when he tried to run. A biter was muzzled, and a stealer of eggs was taught a lesson by being allowed to take an eggshell containing cayenne pepper or a live coal. Worst of all were the dogs who worried sheep or killed lambs or fowl; they were usually very cunning and often escaped detection for a long time. A man in our parish noticed blood on his collie's jowl more than once, but as there was no report of damage in the district he thought it must be from rats or other wild creatures. But one day when he was afoot very early in the morning on the way to Ballybunion for a load of sand, he recognised his own dog running with two others through a field a good fifteen miles from home. On the way home he dropped in to the local pub and led the conversation round to dogs. Yes, there were strange dogs killing sheep in the place, so when he got home he shot the dog at once, and on opening its stomach, there was sheep's wool to prove the case. This post mortem examination was always carried out if a suspected dog was killed. If the owner of the sheep followed the dog to its home and demanded its death, the dog's stomach was opened; if the wool was there, the dog's owner had to pay for the sheep, if not the accuser had to pay compensation for the dog – such was the unwritten law.

Before Louis Pasteur's great work in the 1880s, the thought of a mad dog brought terror. Any dog giving signs of madness was killed at once, and if one escaped and ran away he was chased from parish to parish until he was cornered and put out of misery and public danger. Another unwritten law of the countryside demanded that on the cry of 'Mad Dog!' active men must drop their work and go in pursuit as far as the next village or townland where other men would take up the chase. For those bitten the only known cure was the searing of the fresh wound with a hot iron, and this was one of the most unpleasant duties of the blacksmith. Then the poor wretch must be watched continuously until all danger of infection was past, and if he developed the disease he must be tied up so that he could not harm others until his certain death. Many stories were told of people bitten, of the valiant blacksmith who killed a mad dog to save some children, but was himself bitten; he forged a leg iron and chained himself to his own anvil, so that when he went mad he could harm nobody. And of the woman in a certain village who became so dangerous after a bite that she was suffocated between feather ticks by the terrified neighbours. In actual fact the number of deaths from rabies was small; during the Famine decade, 1841 – 1851, when all sorts of diseases were rife, only four people in the City and County of Limerick died of it, and this was regarded as exceptionally high.

Some people were held to have the gift of training dogs while others 'might as well be idle' for all they could do. The best trained dog was the most valuable, and the man who could teach his dog some unusual trick was greatly admired. In our area there were no sheep, and the polished skill of the trained sheepdog was practically unknown, but good cattle dogs were much sought after, and the man who could train a pup to handle cattle surely and gently had many requests for pups and for the coaching of young dogs. But the unusual trick got the most praise, and in our district the palm went to the man who had succeeded in teaching his dog to bring a half-burned sod of turf from the kitchen hearth to the garden when he wanted a light for his pipe. One day some neighbours put this to the test; the dog was sent off to the house but was long in returning. But the owner told them to wait and see, and soon the dog appeared, walking backwards because there was a strong wind against him which would blow sparks in his face if he trotted as he usually did.

The Horseman's Word

One summer evening long ago I assisted at the burial of an old horse. My assistance, I must admit, was of the literal form of standing by, hindering the work with a small boy's endless questions, but the young farmer who was digging the big hole in which to bury the faithful old mare which had served his father for many years was, I think, glad of a child's chatter which to some degree took his mind away from the sad thoughts brought on by the death of his old friend. A tinker stopped on the road and climbed over the fence to see what was going on, but his first question got a very different answer to mine. 'Why' says he, 'don't you skin her? Wouldn't you get the price of a good few pints for the skin?' Never have I seen such disgust and contempt as came over the young man's face. 'That's enough of that talk, my *buachaill*! She was the good horse to me and mine with that skin on her, and she'll keep it to the last. Didn't I learn to ride on her and I only four years old? Be going with yourself, my man, or maybe 'tis more than talk you'll get from me!' Later I heard the young man's indignant account to his father. 'Don't mind them tinkers!' was the old man's comment 'Some of them would skin yourself for the price of a pint of porter. But it was a good thing that you kept your hand from him, although it would be hard to blame you if you gave him a soho with the handle of the shovel!' All of which is very typical of the Irish countryman's attitude towards his horses, and, we must remember, the tinker who insulted the dead mare was an unusual specimen of his tribe, for many of the travelling folk were expert in the care and the coping of horses.

Nobody can say for certain when the first horses came into Ireland. More than likely they were brought in by warriors rather than by farmers, for the fearless horsemen who wrought such disturbance in the ancient world, the Scythians and the Celts, the Arabs and the Mongols, did much more to spread the horse through Europe, Asia and north Africa than did any plodding race of tillers of the soil. It is probable that their general introduction to Ireland should be credited to the men who made and used the bronze swords which appeared in Ireland about twentyfive centuries ago. The strange blending of wonder-tale and half forgotten history which forms our earliest literature is full of the trampling of horses' hooves, Cúchulain's mighty pair of chariot horses, Grey Macha and Black Seanglan, the Giolla Deacair's strange nag which grew longer and longer as more and more of the warriors of the Fianna mounted until a full fourteen of them were stuck by magic to the ungainly creature's back, the demon horses sighted by Maol Duin in distant ocean islands, Saint Colmcille's old white horse in Iona. Our old folk tales, too, are seldom without horses helping the hero to perform difficult feats and rescuing lovely princesses from pursuing giants. The love of horses and the lore of horses has been part of our tradition for a very long time.

We were always told that horses, in common with the other animals, had human speech in the days before the Flood, and that although they had lost speech, the horses still could understand human speech. In our part of Ireland one says 'Go on!' to a horse to make him go forward 'Wee!' to tell him stop and 'Set!' to get him to back, and as a proof of the horse's power of language we were told how a certain Englishman who happened to be in the locality could not get the horses to understand his peculiar dialect, which had 'Gee hup!' 'Woe!' and 'Back Up!' instead. The sensible animals ignored these foreign expressions and just stood there until someone came who spoke their own language. And as further confirmation we were assured that 'behind in west Kerry all the horses know Irish' by people who had met Gaeltacht farmers at the horse fairs, and heard them gentling their animals in that language. Of course we all know that 'you should talk to a horse the same as if he was a Christian.'

Horses are lucky animals. If a mare drops her seventh foal in the open and you search the place you will be sure to find a four leaved shamrock which will save you from magical and other deceptions. For some reason or other it was held, however, in some parts of Ireland that a foal born at Whitsuntide would turn out vicious and be almost sure to kill somebody sooner or later.

The horse, we were told, could see a ghost much more easily than a human could, and there were many stories of encounters with ghosts and other spirits in which the horse gave a timely warning to his rider and so brought him safe from the uncanny visitant. Here we can be sure that many a horse that shied at a sheet spread on a hedge to dry and left out all night was credited with saving his rider from the unseen world. There were places along the roads where in the past some dreadful deed had been done, and at such places a sensitive horse would baulk and have to be coaxed past the evil spot. There was a postern gate in a demesne wall at Elm Hill near Ardagh in County Limerick which had this sinister reputation, and many people still alive will remember how no horse would willingly pass by it on the road. Often a local man would come upon a stranger in difficulty there and show him how to coax the horse over the invisible obstacle by spreading something – a rug or a sack or a *beartán* of hay or straw or even a handful of grass on a certain part of the roadway. And a tragic story was told to explain why this was so, a tale which tells of a wild and cruel landlord who lived in the big house. One evening, the story runs, this landlord and his dissolute companions were carousing through the district and they abducted a poor girl and dragged her away to the big how where they locked her in a room. While they were still drinking and gambling she escaped through a window, but the alarm was raised and the drunken crew rushed out, mounted their horses and set off in pursuit, and just at the ill-omened spot on the roadway outside the postern gate the landlord, who was leading the chase with loud cries of 'Tally-Ho!', rode her down and she was killed by the horse's hooves. Whether it was deliberate murder or drunken accident the old people could not say, but it was not the fault, they all agreed, of the innocent horse, and ever after any horse that came that way would show his horror of the deed by refusing to pass the cursed place.

The buying and selling of horses were serious matters and the great horse fairs were very important occasions, especially in the old days when cavalry officers from Britain and many of the European countries were there to buy remounts for their regiments and chargers for generals and other mighty men. We are told than Napoleon's famous white horse 'Marengo' was bred in County Wexford and bought by a French nobleman who later presented him to the Emperor, and it is said that the charger ridden by Wellington at Napoleon's final defeat at Waterloo was bought at the fair of Cahirmee. We can be sure that Irish horses, like Irish soldiers, left their bones on the battlefields right across Europe from Flanders to the Crimea and even farther afield. It is sad to think of the gentle animals from the wide fields of Tipperary and Kildare or the hill farms of West Cork dying in the blood and smoke of some foolish quarrel between foreign potentates and we may be thankful that this horror, at least, has gone from more recent though not more reasonable wars.

At the horse fair the prospective buyer would look out for the characteristics of a good horse as laid down in the old saying: 'Three traits of a bull, a bold walk, a strong neck and a hard forehead; three traits of a fox, a light step, a look to the front and a glance to each side of the road; three traits of a woman, a broad bosom, a slender waist and a short back; three traits of a hare, a lively ear, a bright eye and a quick run against a hill.'

It was at a fair in Rathkeale that I saw for the first and only time the strange power of the 'horseman's word'. A young colt, either through fear or perverseness, was prancing and kicking wildly when a boy of about seventeen walked in and fondled the horse's nose, talking quietly. Immediately the colt became calm and the boy took the headstall and led him up and down as meek as a lamb. We were told that this boy, the son of an itinerant horse dealer, had the power to calm any horse. Some people said that it was a hereditary secret in his family, others that he had learned it from an old Palatine farmer in the district who also had this strange gift. It was said, too, that as well as being able to quieten horses and break untrained animals in a matter of minutes, this boy could get a horse to stand still and not move for any force or persuasion until he or somebody else who had the power released it. There is no doubt at all that certain persons have this gift, not only in Ireland but all over the world, but no satisfactory explanation is forthcoming. In Ireland it is known as 'cogar i gcluais an chapaill' or simply 'the whisper' and its potency is held to lie in the words which are spoken in the horse's ear. Some authorities hold that it comes from some characteristic of the person himself which is recognised by the horse, others say that it is done by breathing into the horse's nostrils, and still others maintain that the 'whisperer' puts on his hands or his clothes some mysterious substance the smell of which has the desired effect on the horse.

A very famous 'whisperer' lived near Newmarket in County Cork about a hundred and fifty years ago, a workman named Sullivan. He was never known to fail to subdue even the wildest and most vicious horse, even one which had killed others who tried to break it. He always worked in private – his method was secret, and he did not want to reveal it to anybody, not even to his own son who tried to carry on the art after the father's death. Sullivan usually worked the charm in the horse's stable. Often he was told that the horse was violent, and that going into the stable meant certain injury if not death, but he took no notice of the warnings and just walked into the stable and shut the door, and within half an hour he led the horse out, calm and gentle and ready to be handled by anyone. He never used force, and it was remarked that no noise or bustle was heard from the stable while he was employing his art. He was ready to travel around to attend to horses for a guinea or two, and made a modest income in this way, although he could not be persuaded to leave his native district for any length of time, though offered large rewards to do so. If a young horse was shy of being shod, Sullivan held it at the forge and there was no trouble. Once, at a stable near the Curragh he tamed a vicious brute of a racehorse named King Pippin who had the nasty habit, when a stable boy tried to bridle him, of picking him up in his teeth and shaking him as a dog shakes a rat, and in this way injured several men. Sullivan spent a whole night in this horse's box, and in the morning King Pippin was as gentle as a lamb. This horse won several races and remained gentle for over three years but then became vicious again and had to be put down.

This gift was also shared by women. In south Kerry there is a tradition of a girl named Máire O'Beirn whose father owned many horses; she could go up on the mountain where the untried young horses were running wild and walk up to any one of them and, after a few minutes gentling, mount it and ride it back to the stable, completely broken in. That such a valuable gift was kept a secret is not surprising, but nowadays we do not hear of it as often as formerly. Of course our horse population has fallen enormously during the past fifty years. First the coaches and cabs, the phaetons and barouches and all the other fashionable rigs disappeared from the towns and the roads, their place taken by the motor car. Then the drays and carts gave way to the vans and lorries on the streets and roads, and now the traps and sidecars are becoming extinct. Now the working horses are yielding to the tractor, and only on the racecourse and the hunting field is the horse still unchallanged. A hundred years ago the horse was familiar to everyone in town as well as in country, while more and more people nowadays spend their lives without ever having been near a horse. The traditional lore of the horse is dying too, and it may well be that the secret of the 'whisper' will die with it.

The Labouring Man

In those parts of Ireland, chiefly in the West and North-west, where farms are small, the traditional way of work has always been that the farmer and his family did the work of the farm without hired labour, and when a big day's work, such as drawing the turf or getting in the hay, was to be done, the neighbours gathered in a *meitheal* to do it, and each farmer had a circle of friends to whom he, in his turn, went on the day of their *meitheal*. In those districts there were very few men who depended entirely on paid agricultural labour for their living. There was quite a different pattern of work, say fifty years ago, in the dairy farming districts of Munster, where the farmers depended upon the employment of the 'servant boy' and the 'servant girl' for the running of the farm. These were mostly unmarried men and women, usually in their 'teens or twenties, who were engaged for the year or the season and were given food and lodging on the farm. Very many of them were the sons and daughters of small holders from west and south Kerry, who came in the spring, around Saint Patrick's Day, to Tralee or Newcastle West, Kilmallock or Cashel, and were hired until Christmas on terms settled at the time of hiring. Most of them were thrifty souls, and allowed the greater part of their wages to accumulate until the end of their term so that they could carry it back home with them. Usually there were good relations between the master and the servant boys and girls, and these came back year after year to the same farm, or sent their younger brothers and sisters or other young friends to take their places when they moved on to some other employment. Sometimes it happened that the farmer, or worse still, his wife, was of a mean nature, and skimped on the food and lodging, and many tales were told in the west of the encounters with misers of this kind, like that of the kindly farmer who saw one of the boys not eating his supper. 'What is wrong with you, *a gharsúin*?' 'Oh, sir, 'tis how I'm afraid I'm loosing the sight of my eyes!' 'And how do you make that out, boy?' ''Tis how the missus says the bread is buttered and I can't see a pick of butter on it!' Whereupon the farmer told his wife to butter the bread for the boy. 'How is the eyesight now, boy?' 'Greatly improved, sir, for I can see the cut of bread as clear as anything through the butter!' Needless to say, the bad repute of such farms got around, and they found it not so easy to get servants in the future.

It was, naturally, in the areas of big farms that labourers were most in demand. Some of these were in regular employment on the same farm year in year out, and this was especially the case with herdsmen, ploughmen and carters who were expert in particular jobs and, a very important point, used to the handling of animals. Many of these men had followed their fathers and even grandfathers on the same farm, and usually they had a house on the farm or close by, and often had other perquisites too, such as a garden, the grass of a cow or the right to cut turf in the bog, and frequently their wives and older children had regular or occasional work on the farm. They were poor people, indeed, but their lot was not a hard one; there usually was mutual trust and sympathy between them and the master, their future was fairly secure and they could depend on help in time of need. They formed a settled and very necessary part of the rural population.

Another substantial labour force was provided, a century or so ago, and in lessening volume up to the coming of farm machinery, by the migratory labourers from the West, the *spailpíní fánacha* still remembered in ballad and in local tradition. These were small farmers and their sons from the poor lands along the west coast who were enabled by the mild climate of those parts to plant their own small gardens of potatoes and oats and then move off in groups to find work on the spring planting inland. In the Autumn they followed the same pattern; as soon as their own small harvests were in, they took to the road again, each man with his scythe or his reaping hook carefully wrapped in hay-rope, to reap and mow the wide fields of the lowlands. The men from west Munster usually found employment in east Munster and Leinster, but the men from west Mayo and Donegal went farther afield to England and Scotland. Good workmen went back year after year to the same farm where they were well known and their strength and skill valued. There were, in the large farm areas, others, local men who were known experts at mowing, fencing or draining, and who because of their skill were sure of good employment, moving round the district from one farm to another as their services were required. These often were hired by piecework, so much for mowing a five-acre field, so much a perch for building a fence, scouring a dyke or digging a drain.

In the nineteenth century and on into the twentieth, you could find these various types of farm workers in almost any part of the large farm areas of western Europe. But in the Ireland of the early nineteenth century there was another large class of the rural population whose lot was neither secure nor happy. These were the people who had neither holdings of land nor settled employment, and they were very numerous in the years preceeding the Great Famine of the late 1840s. Their existence presented a very serious social problem at the time, and the British Government carried out several detailed enquiries into their conditions, without, unfortunately, ever doing anything significant to relieve the situation.

The movement towards Irish independence which gave rise to the Irish Volunteers of 1782 and the achievements of Grattan's parliament brought about increased activity in both agriculture and industry, and in those days, especially on the land, there was work for every willing pair of hands. Agricultural methods still depended almost entirely on manual labour, and even though ploughs were reasonably common, many farmers found it more economical to till even the largest fields by digging with the spade rather than by ploughing and consequently more and more labourers were needed. Even after the Act of Union which came into force in 1801 and deprived Ireland of any vestige of self government, the wars between Britain and France continued the demand for Irish agricultural produce of all kinds, prices remained high and employment on the land secure. But the defeat of Napoleon at Waterloo in 1815 brought an inevitable reaction, and Irish industry and agriculture began to feel the pinch. Many labourers on the land who hitherto had enjoyed constant employment now found themselves redundant, not sure of enough casual employment to support themselves and their families, and their numbers were swelled by the many workers in small industries which had failed, and by the return of the thousands of men who had joined the British army to fight in the wars.

Great numbers of these poor people left the country, many to America but in the main to the expanding industrial towns of Britain, where they had to take up the crudest and lowest paid forms of labour. But very many tried to hold on and make a living as best they could. Occasionally some public work such as roadmaking, drainage or the building of harbours gave them hope for some time, but these invariably came to an end, and they were again unemployed. From time to time there was casual labour with the farmers, but this was seldom of long duration; the farmers often found it hard enough to keep on their own trusted workmen, and often had to let even these go to swell the labour-hungry mass. Many workers became nomads, moving here and there with their families, getting a job for a day or a few days here and there and then having to move on, often trying to keep body and soul together by begging. The farmers did their best for them; thousands of pounds' worth of food was handed out at the farmhouse doors – an enquiry in the 1830s estimated the value of this at no less than one million pounds yearly.

It was already the custom in many parts of Ireland that a farmer would permit a labourer to have a small piece of ground, say a half-acre, on which he could build a little cabin and grow potatoes to support himself and his family, and the usual rent was so many days' work in the year. This custom was intensified by the great surplus of labour in the 1820s and 1830s and many farmers let in poor people in this way more out of compassion than from any material advantage. Another custom, already known but becoming more and more common about this time was that called 'conacre', 'rood-land', 'quarter-ground' and other names, which consisted of the renting of a piece of land for the term of the growing season. A man took, say, half an acre of ground on rent from the farmer and tilled it, planted a crop and harvested it, hoping to make a good profit. In normal times this was a reasonable speculation for a small farmer, or for a labourer who could take time off to work his conacre. In a bad year he might have little or no profit, but in a good year he would add very usefully to his income. But in the 1820s and 1830s very many poor men took concacre as their only means of livelihood. The demand was great and the rents consequently high, often allowing only a slight margin in a good year. In County Limerick such land was known in Irish as 'talamh scóir', and the small house built by the poor man who staked his all on it a 'bothán scóir'. In most cases the rent of this ground was reckoned in money, and figures show that it was often five or six times as much per acre as the rent paid by the farmer to the landlord. But usually the farmer was content to take a part of the crop equivalent to the rent in payment, or in some cases to allow the workman to repay some of the rent in day labour.

Shortly before the famine, the number of people who

depended upon such precarious means for a living had increased so much as to make up almost a quarter of the rural population of Ireland. We are told that they were – as we may well imagine – lacking in responsibility. That, for instance, they married young and with little thought for the future – 'If a labourer gets a quarter of ground he thinks he has made a proper provision for marriage; a labourer asked me to lend him £2 to pay for his wedding... he said that he had got a quarter of an acre from a farmer and could therefore keep a wife.' And this was at a time when the marriage of a farmer's son or daughter was the subject of much negotiation about the fortune and the number of cows on the farm.

This could not go on. The famine of Black '47 pressed heavily on the farmers, but most of them survived into better times, but the casual labourers and the poor conacre people went down before it in thousands. Housing statistics included in the Census returns show that while the number of farmhouses, large and small, increased, if only slightly, in the famine decade, more than three hundred thousand small one-roomed cabins were swept from the land. Ever afterwards the landless labourer was, as he still remains, only a small minority of the rural population.

Tall Ships

A look at a picture of any of our seaports as it was during the last century will show us something not to be seen there now and never to be seen again. All down the quaysides and out in the river or inlet is a forest of the masts and spars of dozens of sailing ships. In the early years of the century, about a hundred and fifty years ago, sail was still supreme on the seas; the steamship was still very much a dream of the future. Even a hundred years ago the windjammer still held its own, and it was not until the early years of our own century that mechanically driven ships had really begun to push the sailing ship off the highways of the ocean. Yet today the children growing up in many a seaside town and parish have never seen a sailing ship and the chances are that they never will set eyes on that lovely sight – a tall ship driving along under full sail.

A hundred years ago there were over a thousand ships registered in Irish ports. Of these a small number were steamships and very many were very small craft engaged in coasting trade, but there were some hundreds of deep water sailing ships, from full-riggers of over a thousand tons to schooners of a hundred tons or so, trading to all parts of the world. Even the little ships made very long voyages, and there was hardly a port in any of the six continents which did not know Irish ships and Irish seamen. A typical run for a schooner of 150 tons or so might go like this: Waterford to Cardiff with provisions in casks; Cardiff to Cadiz with coal; Cadiz to Newfoundland with salt for the great fisheries of the Grand Banks; Newfoundland to Italy with salt codfish; Sicily to Spain with sulphur; Spain back to Waterford with a cargo of oak bark for the tanneries. Such was the life of many of the ships, tramping from port to port, picking up a cargo wherever it could be found and carrying it anywhere it was required. Other ships had more regular runs. There was a whole fleet of colliers bringing coal from the Welsh and English coal ports. Some of these were quite big boats which came regularly to Dublin, Belfast, Cork and the larger ports, but others were little schooners and brigs supplying the local markets and calling at Skibbereen, Dungarvan, Ballyvaughan, Tarbert, Belmullet, Killybegs, Rathmullen and other small ports, and to little quays and piers which have not seen a vessel of any sort for the last fifty years. There were big vessels, fully rigged ships, barques and barquentines bringing wheat from Australia and Canada or guano from the Pacific coast of South America or tea from Canton; on the outward voyage they carried butter and beef in casks and firkins. Another notable grain trade was to the Black Sea, to Varna, Odessa and Galatz for wheat and maize; in parts of the south east of Ireland you can still hear maize called 'galatz', a survival of the days when the mouth of the Danube was as familiar to Wexford sailormen as the bar at the mouth of their home port. More maize came from the eastern ports of the United States, and often the outgoing ships carried a full complement of emigrants trying their fortune in the New World. Another now almost forgotten trade was the carrying of provisions, tallow and candles to the West Indies and bringing back rum, coffee and sugar. Other vessels took provisions, hides and woollen goods to the eastern Mediterranean and loaded oranges and dried fruits for the home run, while others carried salt and smoked herrings to the Baltic ports and brought back tar, hemp and timber. Along the quaysides and in the taverns of Arklow and Limerick and Waterford you could hear familiar talk of Charleston, Havana and Valparaiso, of Sydney and Macao, of Smyrna, Genoa and St. Petersburg, and those who could boast only of passages to Liverpool or Bordeaux were only small fish beside the far-faring men who had run the Strait of Malacca or rounded the Horn.

In the foaming waves of the sailors' talk you could hear the names of many a famous ship. Somebody might recall the tale of the *Ouzel Galley* that sailed from Dublin for the Levant in 1695 and was taken by the Barbary Pirates who made slaves of the crew and forced them to work the vessel in many pirate raids, until, one dark night, the crew broke loose and killed their captors and sailed the ship back to Dublin laden with the rich hoard of the pirates. Then it was that the row and the ruction began. The ship had been insured and the owners, believing that she had been completely lost, had claimed, been paid and (worst of all) spent the insurance money. After long discussion it was decided that the unexpected wealth should be applied to the benefit of shipping in general, and the result was the beginning of the Dublin Chamber of Commerce. Let us hope that the valiant crew were not forgotten in the share-out.

We can be sure, however, that the sailors' talk was more on ships they knew and voyages they had made rather than on any old tale of long ago. There was boasting of fast passages, like that of the brigantine *Clara* which sailed from St. John's, Newfoundland, to Cork with a cargo of salt codfish in 1862 in ten days, a run which would do credit to the steamships of the time and of which many a steamship would not be ashamed today. There were tales of bad weather and contrary winds and of long weeks of tossing about and getting nowhere. One of my grand-uncles, a Fenian who had carried his long muzzle-loader to the attack on Kilmallock barracks in '67 and then had to go on his keeping, spent eleven miserable and hungry weeks in a schooner running from Fenit to Boston; he had brought his food – bread, oaten meal, bacon, tea and sugar – enough for six weeks, and still had some over when he landed, for, as he often explained, he was seasick most of the time and could eat next to nothing. The worst of it all, he said, was being constantly wet with sea-water, with no chance to dry his clothes in the perpetual damp and cold. Well, he could leave the ship at Boston, where he had relatives and a welcome before him, but what about the poor sailors who had to endure months of this on short rations? It was even worse in a vessel becalmed in the tropics, on the usual rations of hard tack and salt horse (ships' biscuit and beef to you land-lubbers, biscuits that were as hard as slates and had to be banged on the table to knock out the weevils before you ate them, and pickled beef that might have been two years in the cask) with the drinking water running short and the pitch bubbling in the deck seams with the heat. No wonder that boils and gurry-sores and scurvy plagued the unfortunate crew, and that many a good man went overboard sewn in his hammock with a lump of the ballast at his feet to carry his poor corpse down into the deeps below the ranging ground of the sharks.

On the quays of Wexford you might meet a veteran of the barque *Menapia* which used to trade for palm oil in the Bight of Benin in West Africa. She loaded up with brightly coloured cotton cloths, mirrors, trinkets and brass rings, axes, nails and ancient muskets and bartered these for palm oil and copra and maybe an odd tusk of ivory. The local chiefs were friendly enough, although there still was the danger of being mistaken for slave traders, but there were worse enemies than men on that coast, and more than one Wexfordman died of malaria or yellow fever contracted in the mosquito infested African river mouths. Then there was the iron schooner *Cymric* of Arklow in the wine trade with Portugal. During the first Great War the British admiralty took over this ship for naval service and fitted it out as a 'Q-ship', with concealed guns, to hunt German submarines. After the war she was returned to Arklow and continued in peaceful trading, but not without incident, for she ran aground off the Saltees in 1923 and again ten years later on the Wexford harbour bar where she stuck for a week before being towed off. Her unique exploit, however, was a collision with a tramcar. This happened on Ringsend Bridge when one of the Dublin United Tramway Company's cars was passing over and was stabbed amidships by the schooner's bowsprit, and more than one joke about 'three sheets in the wind' was cracked at her expense. This gallant little ship disappeared with all hands on the way from Dublin to Lisbon in 1944, a time of extra peril on the seas, what with floating mines, prowling submarines and trigger-happy airmen on the loose.

With badly lighted coasts, poor navigational equipment and the fury of the elements against ships without engines, there were very many shipwrecks. Hardly a winter passed without its victims, and the sudden storm brought the end of many a good little ship, and many a good big one too. Sometimes the crew were lucky and came safe, sometimes at least a few of them made the shore, but too often 'lost with all hands' was the sailor's requiem. Saddest of all it was when a crowded emigrant ship or a transport packed with soldiers went down. When the English troopship *Seahorse* went down in Tramore Bay in January 1816, when on the way back from the wars, 363 people were drowned, including 71 women and children of the soldiers' families. There was even greater loss of life in the two troopships wrecked just outside Dún Laoghaire on the way to the Peninsular War, and very many of the drowned soldiers were Irishmen who had taken the shilling to fight Napoleon. The inhabitants of Kilkee watched in helpless horror while the emigrant ship *Intrinsic* was driven by a storm under Look-Out Cliff and smashed to pieces. In any seaport town you could hear mournful ballads of shipwreck:

'On the twenty seventh of April from Liverpool set sail
The gallant ship *Pomona* with a sweet and pleasant gale,
Bound for the land of plenty, for 'Freedom!' was her toast,
And nothing interrupted her 'til on the Wexford coast...'

The *Pomona* went aground in a storm near Wexford in April 1859; she was bound for America with passengers, many of them Irish emigrants. There were nearly 400 souls on board, and very few were saved:

'The fate of these poor passengers was dismal for to see.
On bended knees they met pale death and wide eternity.'

During the second World War the last of the Irish sailing ships proved their worth when the country was desperately short of shipping. The end of the war saw a bare dozen still afloat under the Irish flag, and the last rally of sail in Ireland was when the film 'Moby Dick' was being made at Youghal and the film company needed ships for the harbour scenes. Since then they have nearly all gone. Some broken up because of their age, like *Harvest King* of Arklow, some sold, some lost like the lovely little schooner *Antelope* which ran aground in a storm on Dollymount strand – the children play yet around her broken timbers, sticking up through the sand. She was built in Wexford in 1886 from the salvaged timbers of the American ship *Antelope* which was wrecked on the Saltees, and she voyaged to the West Indies, the Black Sea and Newfoundland. Ten years ago there were still

four or-five sailing from Arklow, the last Irish port to
send out sailing ships. Now, if you are lucky, you may
see the last lone survivor coming in to New Ross. Soon
only the ghosts of the windjammers will be sighted off
our coasts, and the fishermen will take warning and stay
in harbour that day.

The Currach Men

On the second of October, 1907, the French windjammer
Leon XIII, 165 days out of Portland, Oregon, with a
cargo of wheat for Limerick, was driven by a gale past
the mouth of the Shannon and into the dangerous waters
of Mal Bay. All along the coast hereabouts are reefs and
rocks and a constantly breaking surf which gives Mal Bay
its old traditional name of *Cuanta na Mara Báine*, the
White Sea Coves, and many a good ship met her end there
in the old sailing days. The *Leon XIII* was a good ship
of over 2,000 tons and well manned by a crew of 25, but
their best efforts failed to keep her off the rocks and she
struck close to Sugar Island not far from the shore. The
local people could see the sailors clinging to the rigging,
but the lifeboat failed to reach them and the vessel began to break up in the battering waves. Night came, and
the next day, and still the lifeboat could do nothing, and
some of the crew, in despair, made a small raft and set
out for the shore only to be capsized. At this stage the
Quilty fishermen took a hand by launching six three-
man currachs or 'canoes' as they are called locally. One
canoe capsized and broke up but its crew were saved by
their comrades, as were the French sailors in the water
and on the ship. The bravery of the fishermen was
praised on all sides and money from France was subscribed
to build a church at Quilty in memory of the rescue.
Much praise, too was given to the fishermen's boats which
had made the rescue possible in seas in which few types
of boat could live.

These boats are made of tarred cloth stretched on a
wooden framework. They are, of course, very vulner-

able; the least touch of a rock, or even of a sharp drifting spar, can hole the canvas or stave in the fragile ribs. But they are very fast in the water, very easy to handle and very seaworthy. On the water they are easily known even at a distance by their light motion gliding over the waves. On the land they are equally conspicuous, for they are always laid bottom upwards and look like huge black fish; they are never beached and dragged up like a wooden boat, but lifted from the water by two or three men and carried to their stands; one of the familiar sights of our west coast is a currach being marched along like a big beetle, the heads of the bearers hidden inside the upturned hull and the six legs walking in step below. All down the west coast, from Fanad in Co. Donegal to Dingle Bay there are hundreds of these craft still in use, although there were at least twice as many fifty or sixty years ago. Primarily they are fishing boats, and because of their lightness, shallow draught and ease in handling they are perfectly suited to lighter kinds of fishing, such as hand lines, spillyards, light nets and lobster pots. For dwellers in islands they are a godsend, and the people who lived in the Blasket, Iniskea, Inishmurray, as well as those who still live in Tory, Arranmore, the Aran Islands, Scattery and a dozen other islands are as familiar with them as we are with bicycles.

They vary a lot in size from place to place, and there are differences, too, in shape and make. The canoes that rescued the crew of the *Leon XIII* were twenty feet long and a little over three feet wide, gently rounded underneath without any keel so that they slide over the water instead of cutting through it. The father and mother of all Irish currachs might be seen until quite recently in use by salmon fishermen on the river Boyne a couple of miles above Drogheda. These were very simple craft, merely a wicker basket with a hide stretched over it, but they were made with great skill and care by experts in whose families the craft had come down for long centuries. A few of the good old make still survive, and when we examine them we can only wonder at the combination of simplicity and competence which they show.

In making one of them the builder first marked out an oval 6 feet long and 4½ feet wide on the ground with a piece of string and a couple of sticks. Next he got 32 hazel rods 10 feet or more in length and stuck these firmly into the ground at equal intervals all around the oval. Then he wove strong rods through these along the surface of the ground so that they were all held in a band of wickerwork. Next the long rods were bent over to meet and be bound side by side in pairs to form strong double ribs; eight from one long side to meet eight from the other, and seven to meet seven from each end, while the two remaining rods gave strength at the ends. This frame was weighted down with stones so placed as to give the true form needed and left for several days to set, and when the desired shape was fixed all the crossing points in the ribs were tied securely with strong twine. Up to this stage an onlooker might well imagine that the builder was making some outsize type of basket, but the next move would both clear his doubts and add to his puzzlement, for the framework was pulled from the ground and covered with the tanned skin of a large cow or bullock. The hide was made soft and pliable by a good soaking in water and was stretched tightly over the 'basket' and laced all around the edge with strong twine. Then, after some trimming and tightening, a seat was put in place and the currach was ready for launching. Usually two men worked it in the water, one kneeling in front and wielding a paddle while the other sat on the seat facing backwards and handling the net. For an unskilled person the Boyne currach was even more unmanageable than other kinds of boat, but the local fishermen handled them with such skilful ease that it all looked very simple until you tried your hand at it and one of the fishermen had to come to your rescue.

The history of these currachs is as old as that of Ireland itself; the earliest writings which have come down to us are full of references to them. Strange warriors come in them from distant lands. Sinners are required to launch out in a currach made of one hide and let themselves drift at the mercy of God, and saints set forth in them to seek the solitude of lonely islands or to bring the gospel to heathens. Some of them were much larger than the little Boyne craft; we read that the hero Tadhg Mac Céin built a great currach which had twenty five seats and was covered with forty hides, and that Saint Brendan made a voyage in a currach which carried ten people with forty days' provisions. That the knowledge and use of such large wicker, skin-covered boats continued down to much more recent times we know from the account of the retreat of O'Sullivan Beare in 1602. The harried lord of Bearehaven and his little band of fugitives were cut off by the Shannon near Portumna and escaped across the river by killing their horses and making two hide-covered currachs, one small, like the Boyne currachs and the other twenty six feet long and six feet wide. The man who directed the making of the big boat was O'Sullivan Beare's brother Dermot, and it was Dermot's son, Don Phillip, who wrote a full account of the affair, in which he describes the method used – marking out the outline on the ground and making the framework of long rods in the same way as that employed by the currach makers of Oldbridge on the Boyne in the present century.

Traditions from the past and a few descriptions written down a century or more ago leave no doubt that the sea-going currachs of the west coast were formerly covered with animal skins, usually cow-hides, and that the canvas or calico now used to cover the currachs is a recent substitute. In the same way, the framework of hazel rods is known to have been used, in some cases until quite recently, along the west coast. Nowadays, however, the framework is always of wooden laths and the covering is tarred cloth in all the different types from the paddling currachs of North Donegal, which are about 8 feet long and 3½ feet wide to the finest of all boats of this kind, the *naevóg* of the Dingle Peninsula. Curiously enough there is no old tradition of currachs around Dingle, and we are told by Tomás Crohan in his book *An tOileánach*, which has been put into English under the title *The Islandman*, that only wooden boats were used in his early days, and that he well remembered seeing the first currach to come to the district and marvelling at it. This recent introduction, and the necessity of starting a local trade in *naevóg*-making, may be part of the reason why the craft reached such a pitch of perfection here, for there is no denying that the *naevóga* of the Dingle Peninsula are not only the best and most seaworthy of all, but are also the most carefully made and finely finished, the best proportioned and the most elegant looking. They are usually 26 feet long and 4½ feet wide in the middle but ride so lightly on the water that a depth of two feet from the level of the gunwale to that of the bottom is sufficient to keep them well clear. There are no ugly angles anywhere, everything is smoothly curved; the stern narrows to a little transom and the bow rises high out of the water. There are four seats for four oarsmen, each of them pulling a pair of oars, and like nearly all currachs of the western Irish coast, the oarblades are no wider than the shafts, about 2½ inches wide for an oar length of 11 feet. These oars are not 'feathered' when rowing; they pivot on a single pin which passes through a hole in a boss of wood attached to the back of the oar. But the Dingle *naevóga* differ from most others in that they are fitted with a mast and sail which are used when the wind is favourable.

For many years these *naevóga* were the Blasket Islanders' only link with the mainland, and were used not only for fishing but for carrying all sorts of goods in and out. They brought the people to mass and to market, and carried the summer visitors out to the friendly homes of the Island. A cow or three or four sheep were often brought in or out, their legs tied together, lying on a soft pile of seaweed to spare both the animal and the boat. This carrying of animals was not without its dangers. A Donegal writer of a hundred and thirty years ago tells of how a couple of men brought a spancelled bull in a currach from one of the islands. The bull's feet came loose and it would have sunk the currach and drowned the men if one of them – a powerful man apparently – had not muzzled it with his hat, which he squeezed over its mouth and nostrils until it suffocated. The same writer tells of another man who loaded a currach with turf on top of which he first seated his wife and then got his horse to climb up on top and stand on the turf. Then he set out for the mainland and all went well until the horse fell overboard, but the currach man, nothing daunted, actually succeeded in getting the horse back into the currach and up on the turf again!

The decline of inshore fishing, the fall of population along the west coast and the abandonment of many of the islands formerly inhabited, all have helped to reduce the number of currachs now in use. Many a little creek and harbour that once knew them well now sees them no more, and it looks as if they, too, must pass away. It seems a pity, however, that they are so little regarded as sporting or pleasure craft. A smaller version of the Dingle Peninsula *naevóg* should make a wonderful lake and river boat, while its lightness should commend itself to voyagers on canals, as it might so easily be lifted out and carried past the locks.

The People of the Sea

The story is told in County Kerry of a young man who never could sleep. Night after night, all through his childhood and youth, the people of the household went to bed while he sat up by the fire or wandered alone abroad, and why this should be so he could never find out, and he grew sad and sullen because he was so different from the others. But one night a poor scholar asked for shelter in the house, and he and the young man sat long over the fire talking, until, in the small hours of the morning the poor scholar was overtaken by weariness from his long travels during the day, and he excused himself, saying that he thought it was time to go to bed. 'You may go to bed, and welcome' said the young man, 'but I'll sit up by the fire, as I do every night because I have never in my life closed my eyes in sleep. And you are a wandering scholar, a man who has seen far places and heard strange things, and, maybe, you might be able to tell me why I am different from everybody else.' The poor scholar remembered a passage in one of his books, and searched in his book bag until he found it. 'Here it is; the learned authors say that the only people who do not sleep are the People of the Sea. Did any of your people belong to the People of the Sea?' 'I do not know' said the young man 'My mother and her family are always living in this place, but I always heard that my father died before I was born, and I do not know who were his people.' And with that he went and woke his mother and asked her about his father, and she told him yes, that his father was a wonderful person who had come out of the sea in the shape of a seal and then changed into a handsome man. The young man thanked the scholar and rewarded him with money. And the next morning the young man said farewell to his mother and all the household and walked down to the shore and into the sea, and a great wave rose, and in the wave was a splendid stately man who stretched out an arm and took the young man's hand in his, and together they vanished under the sea, never to be seen again.

It is not surprising that the man from the sea in this story should have appeared in the shape of a seal, for the seal played a big part in the tales and beliefs of our coast dwellers. We know that there are two kinds of seal on our coasts, but of these the big grey Atlantic seal is much more common on the west coast than the so-called Common seal. Both types have characteristics which, in an element inhabited by fish, set them apart as something remarkable. An ordinary Atlantic seal or a big Common seal is about the same size as a man; they are warm blooded, they have four flippers, they come on shore and lie on the beach or the rocks, they nurse their young, they call to each other and cry out when hurt. Thus they are much more like human beings than are any other dwellers in the sea; why then should some of them not be humans in disguise or under spells?

In the old days people hunted seals on our west coast. Their flesh has, it is said, a fishy taste because they live on fish, but is quite good to eat, and was very welcome in the 'bad times', when seal meat was salted down like bacon in casks and most fishermen's houses in the Islands off the west coast had a flitch or two of seal meat hanging in the kitchen. Its oil, too, was put to use; it burned in lamps and was used to polish boots and preserve leather; it was rubbed to sails and to the woodwork of boats to make them waterproof; it was a much-valued remedy for 'pains in the bones', and some people drank it, like cod liver oil, or dipped their bread in it when they had no butter. The skin was cured and made into bags and shoes, and skins with the fur still on were comfortable floor mats. Leather merchants were glad to buy the skins, while some people made waistcoats of them and the soft white fur of the baby Atlantic seal was used to trim women's clothes. 'No one need be hungry' as an old fisherman said to me, 'while there was a seal cave near him.' But, at the same time, one should be on the alert for signs which might indicate that the intended victim was some sort of magic seal or enchanted human.

A story from south Kerry tells of a man who took his gun and crept down over the rocks to hunt for a seal. Soon he saw two, a mother seal and a very little one, and he took aim at the adult, but before he could fire she turned and spoke to him: 'Hunter, spare me until I feed my little infant!' – 'I'll spare you now and forever' said he and never again did he kill a seal. Another tale is that of the fishermen who had killed a seal and brought it in to the quay to skin it when they heard a voice from the sea calling 'Brother! Where is my brother?', and saw the other seal rising on the waves, calling in vain for the one which had been killed.

Sometimes on fine nights the seals lie in groups on their favourite smooth rocks, uttering long musical moans and wails – the 'song of the seals', which sounds very like the laments raised for the dead in the old days. By careful crawling you can come quite close to them to enjoy the concert, and even to join in the song if you feel moved that way. Seals are rather inquisitive, and if people have not been shooting at them they will come quite close to a boat to see what its occupants are doing, or swim in close to a bathing beach, sometimes to the alarm of the swimmers who are not used to them and do not know that they are generally quite harmless if not disturbed. Naturally, if a seal is attacked he will try to defend himself, and his powerful jaws and sharp teeth can give a very nasty bite. It is said that a seal will not relax his bite until he hears the bone crack, and the men who went into the seal caves to kill them took the precaution of wearing long stockings plentifully stuffed with cinders in the hope that any seal biting a leg would release the hold of his jaws on hearing the crackling of the cinders.

They are said to be very fond of music and may, we are told, be coaxed to the shore by the sound of a song or a musical instrument. The young of the Common seal are able to swim as soon as they are born and may be seen in the water or on the shore with their mothers, and it is said that if you can come close to one of the little ones you can sing it to sleep like a human baby. There is a story of a man who did this, and carried the small seal home to keep it as a pet, for the young Common seal may be tamed easily, unlike the Atlantic seals which are fiercer and whose young are well grown before they venture into the water. On reaching home the man put the baby seal in a box and fed it with cow's milk and it thrived for some days, to the delight of the children. Until one dark night the man heard the sound of, as it were, great bare feet walking about outside the house and a deep gruff voice saying 'Where is Donal? Where are you, Donal?' – upon which the small seal in the box spoke up and said 'There is my father looking for me.' This was too much for the man, who took the baby seal to the door and told it to be off home to his own people as quickly as ever he could and not to be bringing such unwanted visitors to the house.

Nowadays seals are hardly ever hunted on the Irish coast. They do some harm to salmon fisheries and sometimes an angry fisherman or water bailiff will kill one with a rifle, or a so-called 'sportsman' take a potshot at one, usually only wounding it and leaving it to die in pain and hunger. But there are many rocky coves and islands on the west coast where the seals can live undisturbed, even more so since islands like Inismurray, Iniskea, Inishark and the Great Blasket have been abandoned by their human inhabitants and the seals have quietly taken over other caves and inlets. Not that the islanders ever persecuted the seals; in the harder times they hunted them for food, but always had some respect and regard for them. We hear of helpful seals. Once upon a time, we are told, a boat was lost in a fog towards nightfall, and the fishermen were at their wits' end in fear of being driven on the rocky shore when a seal came up quite close to them. One of the men called the seal and handed him a fresh pollock, and the seal ate it and then swam gently along, the boat following, until it reached safe water. Another tale is that of a man who had missed the boat to the market town and was carried there on the back of a friendly seal, who refused any reward except a glass of whiskey.

In some of these stories the seal is really a seal, although with some human characteristics, but in others, like that of the young man who could not sleep, it is really a human being, whether of the land or of the sea, under enchantment. We all have heard of the young man who saw a number of seals coming on to the shore and taking off their sealskins to appear as lovely young women. He stole one of the skins and the girl to whom it belonged had to follow him home where he dressed her in ordinary clothes, on which she forgot about the sea and was happy to live on the land. The young man married her and they had three lovely children, and all went well until the youngest child one day found a strange bundle hidden in the loft and brought it to his mother, who recognised her sealskin and at once remembered her own people and her life in the sea. She said a fond goodbye to the children, put on the skin and slipped under the waves, and came no more to the people of the land, although she often swam on the surface off the shore talking to her children and singing to them. Several families in Ireland and in the west of Scotland trace their descent from this sea-woman, and members of these families are bound in honour never to help in the killing of a seal.

These and similar stories are still told along the edge of the Atlantic, and only a few weeks ago I heard one such story, which I had not heard before, from the Great Blasket. There was a woman of that Island, and her husband died, leaving her helpless with three children, a daughter and two small sons. And she thought she would leave the Island and try to get some way of living on the mainland, and so she did and she and the children were making their way along, doing some work for a farmer here and a housewife there in return for food and lodgings. One day she was near a cove of the sea when the tide was well out and she left the girl to mind the boys while she went down to gather shellfish for their evening meal, and while gathering it she saw a seal lying on the rock, moaning and licking its flipper. Then she saw a great fishbone stuck in a wound in the flipper, and, out of pity, she pulled it out and cleaned the wound. Some years later, still as poor as ever, she called at a large and wealthy house near the sea to ask for work, but the owner said 'Do you not know me? Do you not remember this?' – holding out a hand marked by an old scar. She could not tell who he was, but he assured her that he was the seal whom she had helped, for he had been changed into a seal by an evil old hag, his own aunt. 'And now' said he 'You have a handsome daughter and I have a fine son. And if these two marry, you may live with them in my other fine house. And your two boys will live here with me and be like my own sons.' And so it all was done, and, in the way of all good stories, they lived happily ever after.